A Girl's Guide to Life

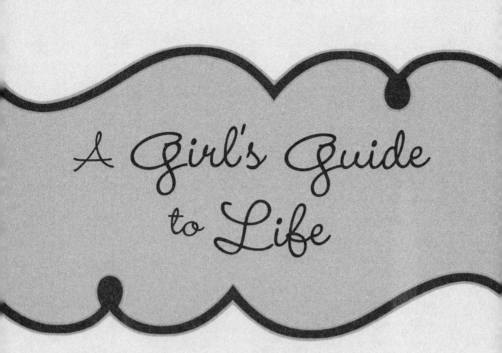

A Girl's Guide to Life

The Real Deal on Growing Up, Being True,
and Making Your Teen Years Fabulous!

KATIE MEIER

THOMAS NELSON

Since 1798

NASHVILLE   DALLAS   MEXICO CITY   RIO DE JANEIRO

Published in Nashville,Tennessee, by Thomas Nelson. Thomas Nelson is a registered trademark of Thomas Nelson, Inc.

Tommy Nelson titles may be purchased in bulk for educational, business, fund-raising, or sales promotional use. For information, please e-mail SpecialMarkets@ThomasNelson.com.

Library of Congress Cataloging-in-Publication Data

Meier, Katie.
 A girl's guide to life : the real deal on growing up, being true, and making your teen years fabulous! / Katie Meier.
  p. cm.
 ISBN 978-1-4003-1594-9 (pbk.)
 1. Teenage girls—Juvenile literature. 2. Adolescence—Juvenile literature. 3. Interpersonal relations—Juvenile literature. 4. Conduct of life—Juvenile literature. 5. Femininity—Religious aspects—Christianity. I. Title.
 HQ798.M453 2010
 305.235'2—dc22

                                                                    2010003836

CPSIA
Mfr: R.R. Donnelly / Crawfordsville, IN / February 2011 - PO# 118298

Contents

Introduction

Welcome to your life, girl! You're growing up, and that means growing better, smarter, older, and embracing life as a young and independent woman.

You know that diary dreaming you do when you fantasize about what it would be like to have that lifestyle, attitude, job, wardrobe, and everything else you hope for in the future? When you write down the kind of qualities you admire in your friends, in other girls you look up to, or even in celebrities? That kind of dreaming is what creates the woman you're likely to be when you grow up. The more active your imagination, the better. It's going to take a lot of practice (and some trial and error) to find out the identity that suits you best.

Whatever kind of girl you dream of becoming, you'll have to develop the strength it will take to get you there. This strength is located in three places: your mind, your body, and your soul.

You'll need your mind to be quick to get the jump on opportunities that interest you, to make good choices, and to figure out difficult challenges so hard times don't creep up and swallow your drive to be your best.

With a mind this sharp, you're gonna need a body to match. Chasing down your dreams and growing into womanhood takes a good bit of effort, and a strong body will get you there, making you feel great along the way.

And last, you'll need the most important thing of all: a good understanding of your own soul. Our souls breathe life into us. They fuel our inner hearts, move our feelings, and whisper answers to us about the big questions in life, like purpose, faith, and belief. Without our souls we'd just be a big jumble of body parts and a brain. But our souls tie these things together, animate our beings, and direct our paths as we look toward the future.

So let's wrap up all this chat and jump right in, okay? Feel free to crack open the book and zip over to the pages you're most interested in or curious about. Anything goes. Each topic is laid out pretty much the same way so you'll get info, answers to questions, and a dose of sisterly advice with every chapter, no matter where you start.

Mind, body, and soul. They're ours, so let's make them a reflection of us. Let's tailor our lives around a clear heart, a creative spirit, and a Christ-infused strength. Onward and upward, gals . . . let's do it!

Part one:
MIND

Chapter 1

Self-Esteem

Pop quiz: Think of five things about you that are great, and write them below.

1. I'm _____.

2. I'm _____.

3. I'm _____.

4. I'm _____.

5. I'm _____.

Okay, if you're reading this sentence and you still haven't written anything down, you're getting a big score of 0. Seriously, you have to go back and give the quiz a shot. Go do it real quick. I'll wait here for you to finish up.

If you're done, here's the deal with the quiz. The basic point of asking any girl to rattle off five great things about herself is to see what's going on inside her mind. It's a quiz that asks a girl to put down on paper what she believes is true about herself.

For girls who have a tough time coming up with answers, this can be a sign of something not too great: low self-esteem.

It can sometimes mean that a girl doesn't know what she's worth in her own mind. It can mean that she has a tough time seeing what's great about herself and an even tougher time telling others about these things.

The "Land of No"

If you asked ten people if you're smart, what's the chance that at least a few of them would say yes? What's the chance they'd say you were pretty? What about athletic, funny, cool, or brave?

If you think the chances are pretty low, you're not alone. Girls who feel like they don't measure up in some way are often the best people to ask about self-esteem. If a girl has felt like this and come out stronger on the other side, she can give us hope. A girl like this can show us what *not* to do with our lives. She can show us where to keep our minds from wandering if we hope to grow into womanhood as confident, strong, and self-assured women.

An author who died in 2002 was a girl like this. Her name was Caroline Knapp. The very last book she wrote was titled *Appetites*. It was a whole book about why women feel like they need to be a certain way or live up to a certain expectation.

Her book made it clear to girls that if they lived in what she called the "Land of No," insecurity and low self-esteem were going to be constant partners in their lives. During our teen years, girls can sometimes spend so much time in the "Land of No" that they forget one little detail: the "Land of No" isn't real at all.

If girls live in the "Land of No," then they're being tricked. They're trapped inside a world that looks real, feels real, but is totally fake. The "Land of No" is a place that we allow our minds to make up and inhabit. If we stay there long enough, the "Land of No" becomes the only place we feel safe living.

The "Land of No" is a place inside many girls. Each girl

might have her own version of it, but the general atmosphere is one of shame. In the "Land of No," girls see themselves, but they see themselves as less than who they really are. They see themselves as incapable. They see themselves as weak, lost, powerless, boring, or less than other people in different ways.

How Girls Get There

Girls who end up in this spiral of shame never really intended to go there in the first place.

Research into what girls are like during different stages of their lives has some interesting things to tell us. For example, think back to when you were only nine or ten. What kind of girl were you? If you were anything like the researchers say, it's a safe bet that you were friendly, liked to learn and try new stuff, were in a pretty good mood, and felt like you could even take on the world sometimes.

But was there a point in your life where you began to change a little bit? Like when you became more worried about what you looked like or what other people thought of you? If so, then you're just about the same kind of girl that these researchers were looking at.

The big-deal find after all their study was that girls change suddenly and dramatically. Girls go from being psyched about the world to being worried about superficial stuff like looks and people's opinions. For most girls, this makes them nervous that they don't measure up. All of a sudden they look in the mirror and start to feel insecure. They look around and worry that they can't compete in terms of smarts, body, friends, hobbies, boys, or talents.

What's happened to girls like this? These girls have entered the "Land of No." Again and again these girls get paralyzed by the worry that they just don't measure up.

No, they're not good enough, they think to themselves.

They're not smart enough.
They're not tall enough.
They're not rich enough.
They're not interesting enough.
They're not athletic enough.
They're not skinny enough.

A Short History of Girls

So let's get some history on this sudden change in the life of a girl. The best place we can start to understand the history of insecurity is the 1950s. Today, in the twenty-first century, the pictures we see of the '50s are almost always used as a joke. Black-and-white photos of a busy mom who's lost in culinary bliss while fixing meatloaf—in her pointy bra, tidy little sweater set, and her matching high heels—look hilarious to us today.

But that was the real deal back in the '50s. Women were the mommies of American culture. Men were the worker bees. Men supported the family. This meant women stayed home, had babies, cleaned the house, raised the kids, and made sure everything was spick-and-span. The ultra-white smile you see so many gals sporting in pictures from the '50s was indicative of how stoked your family was supposed to feel because you were their mom. It was up to you to keep it all running smooth.

This mommy-perfect kind of girl gave way when the 1960s rolled around. This was the hippie generation and the start of women fighting for equal rights all across America. From the street to the workplace, women wanted to be treated the same, paid the same, and given the same chances to succeed. No more making sandwiches and keeping a tidy house for these mamas. They wanted in on the working world of America. And they wanted to be treated equally when they got there.

The 1970s kept women right on rolling with their quest for equality. The '70s gave rise to the movement you may have heard of called "feminism." This movement centered on winning equality for women in lots of different parts of their lives, like getting into politics or making the same kind of money that men make for doing the same job. Feminists worked to give women the right to be themselves, make their own choices, and determine their own futures.

With the feminist movement working toward equality for women, the '70s saw girls split into a few different camps, depending on how they thought women should go about getting equality for themselves. One group of feminists (sometimes called "radicals") thought the best way to go about things was to teach women to get away from thinking girls should do certain things just because they're women. For example, women shouldn't all have to stay at home and be moms. If a girl doesn't want to start a family because she's right in the middle of a killer job, she shouldn't have to, even if she becomes pregnant. And here, in the 1970s, is where the debate around abortion first heated up. Radical feminists were absolutely committed to a girl's right to do what she wanted with her body, no matter what.

Big Myth: Being a girl was easier in the past.

Real Deal: Being a girl has always been an uphill struggle.

Other groups of women still fought for equality but focused on different stuff. These groups of women didn't agree with radical feminist ideas, like the right to abortion; they wanted to zero in on social, not personal, issues. For example, women who wanted to change the world socially fought to get girls admitted to what used to be all-male college institutions, like West Point or the Citadel. These women worked to get girls elected in politics, urged women to educate themselves at higher and higher levels, and encouraged females to start businesses or run large corporations so they could have a say in what went on in society and business.

By the 1980s women were doing many things that used to be boys-only. We were getting into big-time power positions in companies. We were making more money than ever before. We were choosing when and where we wanted to work and what kind of life we wanted to build.

I was only five years old when the 1980s began, but I can tell you that moms like mine were into this idea. My mom spent a few years wearing power suits, stockings, heels, and carrying a fancy briefcase to her big corporate job each day. She also took a shot at being a soccer coach, a Girl Scout leader, a director at our church, and a competitive player on a tennis team. She totally embodied the go-get-'em spirit of women in the '80s. And I loved that about her.

So by the end of the twentieth century, in the 1990s, you'd think that women would be psyched and confident. People like my mom were blazing trails for girls like us to follow when we became women. By speaking out, the ladies that came before us made some serious strides from back in the day when women didn't *choose* to be stay-at-home moms, they were *expected* to. Wasn't this a big victory?

According to psychologist Mary Pipher, the answer just might be no. She wrote a book in the 1990s called *Reviving Ophelia* that told about how the situation for young girls really wasn't getting any better despite all the progress that had been made. Equal rights, equal pay, and an increased sense of independence were all great things. But girls also became part of a more competitive culture.

Because of this, girls face cultural pressures that can force them to split their focus. One half of you wants to stay real and true to who you have always been. The other half tries to be whoever the cultural standards require you to be. This is the half of a girl that's always trying to measure up. This is the half that can wake up insecure and ashamed.

When we look around us, it's easy to see that Mary Pipher was right. As teenage girls in the twenty-first century, we can be more than a little confused about all the different directions our society is pulling us. It's like we're supposed to be everything all at once—beautiful, athletic, career-minded, future "moms of the year," expert chefs . . . you get the point. But, we're only supposed to do all of these things if we do them in certain ways. What's worse is that we're sometimes not even that interested in doing any of it, but if we don't get it done, we fear what could happen. Parents might be mad. We might not get into college. Our friends might think we're lame and ditch us. Or we might not be cool, thin, popular, or fit in anymore.

These pressures are what keep this sense of shame in girls going strong. Because we can sometimes get so confused over what we're supposed to be, we begin to think we're failing at all of it.

Living in Fear

If you're a girl, chances are that you've lived in the "Land of No." You may not have, but you probably will, at least once in your life.

This is the part you can't change. What you can change, though, is the way you respond to those feelings of insecurity. You can understand what it feels like to fall away from your true self. You can understand that what's going on is in your own mind, and it's something you can control.

Falling Away from Your True Self

Feeling confident and proud of your abilities? That's the way it feels when you're using your true self to face the world.

The opposite of this is when you're down, bummed, or worried that you don't measure up. When you feel like this, it can lead you to make choices that you don't really like. You might act in ways that aren't really you. You may dress in styles that are just like everybody else because you're afraid of being rejected. You may agree with stuff you don't believe in, pretend you don't know the answers to questions, or pretend you don't really have an opinion about things so people won't make fun of you.

Either way, when doubt and worry begin to make you act differently than you normally would, you're falling away from your true self. Even the very first time you say *yes* when you really think *no*, you're falling away from that true self. And it's a big deal.

Some girls try to pretend this isn't the case, though. They figure that girls who speak up and do their own thing are just different. They figure that girls like this were just born confident, or something.

Big Myth: Some girls are just born confident.

Real Deal: All girls have confidence within them.

But it's not that you were born without confidence. It's that something has made you question yourself. Something has made you think things like, *I'm not good enough, Other girls are better,* or *I shouldn't even try.*

If you've ever said things like this to yourself, then now is the time to make some changes. Begin to watch your thoughts like a hawk. For example, try counting the number of times in a day that you don't feel good about yourself. Write down the thought you had in your head and the situation that made you feel that way.

Thoughts	Situations
....	....
....	....
....	....
....	....
....	....
....	....

Check out this list at the end of the day. Evaluate which things on the list even really matter. You'll probably find that only a few of them do. Most of the things will probably be superficial stuff like feeling too fat or not feeling cool enough.

Sweating the small stuff like appearance is exactly what drives girls into a spiral of self-doubt. Don't let yourself go there. If you're already at that point, hang a U-turn as soon as you can.

CONTROLLING YOUR MIND

Controlling your thoughts is a powerful way to keep from getting stuck in those nasty feelings of inadequacy. And it starts with controlling what you say.

"Think before you speak." Ever had someone tell you this? It's usually used as a way to scold or tell us to be more considerate about other people. And you know what? That's how we're going to use this saying too. We're going to get into the habit of learning how to be more considerate to someone: us.

The first thing you should know about thinking before you speak is that words have the power to create reality. This is one reason that the "Land of No" exists in the first place. After hearing words that tell you you're not good enough, you end up believing it. Girls create a whole reality where they're not good enough, just because a few words told them so.

Here's a quick list of some words that have become so powerful when girls say them that they make the "Land of No" only a few thoughts away:

You Know? Ending all of your sentences with "you know?" is a way of asking people to agree with you. Most girls who end their sentences this way are looking for acceptance. They want to hear that other people agree with their ideas because hearing this can make you feel accepted or liked. Skip this trap and just say what you've gotta say. Your opinion is good enough all by itself.

I Hate My . . . Hate + you = "Land of No." Why spend time focusing on what you don't like about yourself? Seriously, where does that get any girl? Instead, just know there will always be things about you that are less than ideal. This is just a fact of life. And it's true about everyone. But there's no sense dwelling on these things—they'll always be there. If it's not one thing, it will be another, because girls are always growing and changing who they are. We get tired of some of our parts, and want to change others. So focus on this power of change if you really can't live with some part of yourself. Don't focus on scolding yourself.

I Don't Know. Welcome to the number one smart-girl lie of the century. When you say you don't know as a way to avoid speaking your mind, you're underestimating yourself.

Speaking your mind is a risk. I won't kid you. Is it as risky as trying to live life as a girl who doesn't have a strong body, mind, and soul?

A Way Out

Knowing what kind of words begin to create a sense of insecurity in you is the first step, and we've just checked that out. Now we're ready to figure out how words can empower you in your life. Here are a few ways to find the words that will create a world that's real:

RECOGNIZE CULTURAL PRESSURES

Ask yourself what your culture is asking you to do. For example, when you read magazines, do you feel like you are being asked to look like the girls you see? If so, be sure you realize who or what is doing the asking. Is it you asking yourself to be like this? Or is it a cultural pressure asking you to be this way?

Go with words that are from God, not from the culture around you.

RECOGNIZE GENDER INEQUALITIES

Boys and girls aren't the same, no matter what anybody tells you. Even though ladies since the 1950s have been striving to make the world equal for guys and girls, this just isn't the case. God made us different, with different roles in this world.

Different girls realize this at different times. Some girls realize it when they grow a little bit older and don't end up making the same kind of money as a guy who does the same job in their office. Other girls realize it when they're still in school and have a teacher who treats boys like they're smart and girls like they're pretty.

Use words that don't link gender to success—like saying achievements are good "for a girl." Focus on yourself and what you can do as a *person*, not a *girl*.

STOP THE COULDA-SHOULDA-WOULDA MONSTER

You can't go back. You can't do things over. So why use words that stress what you should have done, could have done, or would have done if you could do it all again?

Moving forward means making things from the past better or different. It doesn't mean erasing them. Use words that allow you to see the future, not dwell on the past.

SPEAK UP AND OUT

Talk to yourself. Talk to others about yourself. Speaking about what you're good at or taking compliments in stride can create a reality where you feel successful. Feeling this way leads to confidence. It leads to a desire to keep learning, growing, and succeeding.

Don't believe you can focus on yourself without feeling like a big snob? Check out Philippians 4:8, a verse that encourages us to focus on things that are admirable and excellent. While it's a bad idea to be a self-centered jerk who makes a habit of broadcasting all your accomplishments, it's a great idea to wrap your mind around admirable and excellent things, especially if they're qualities lying inside of you.

Don't Take No for an Answer

Don't let words create a place in your life where you're not good enough. When you hear this kind of talk, walk away. When you begin to think these kinds of thoughts, cool down and think about what you're saying. Use words that are real. Say the things that you know are true from the Scriptures. Live from your true self, and don't fall away.

Chapter 2

Romance

So you've seen those cheesy ads, I'm sure. You know, the perfume ads filmed in black and white with the guy and girl who are desperately in love, rolling around together in the ocean surf while soft breezes blow their wispy hair all around their faces. Come on. Who does that?

Yeah, the ads are pretty lame. For real, who rides her bike straight into oncoming waves while she's wearing a long, see-through dress?

But as lame as the ads can be, they're also pretty serious. The ad is piling up all kinds of references to things we find romantic just to sell a product. Like if the images in the ad remind us of things we love, the idea is that we will think we love their newest perfume (or whatever product they're selling) too. The whole deal is about hitting people who watch straight in the heart. It's all about making us feel the romance.

For girls today, romance can sometimes seem like something from the past. Things that used to be considered romantic—like a guy opening a car door, pulling out a chair from a table, or just generally saving a "damsel in distress"— can seem downright sexist today. Guys who do stuff like this risk being called *pigs, jerks,* or *misogynists* (miss-soj-a-nists) because they just won't butt out and let girls do their own thing.

What's a girl to do? It's no lie to admit that a lot of modern girls still go home and dream about a Prince Charming. Wishing a guy would sweep us off our feet might be old-school for modern girls like us, but it's a dream that's still alive. It's a dream in the hearts of tons of girls, all over the place.

This dream is exactly what reality TV shows like *The Bachelor* are all about. Even though this is the twenty-first century, you can count on getting a whole line of girls who will risk public humiliation for a chance to be swept off their feet— even by a complete stranger. And it's not like the girls who audition are flaky do-nothings. You've got lawyers, businesswomen, nurses, and teachers all lining up for a shot at Prince Charming himself.

So the first thing we're going to do in the romance chapter is figure out what kind of girl we are, anyway. Are we the hopelessly romantic type? Or, are we more of a mix of romantic heart and modern head? Check out the two lists below and match up your real feelings about romance.

10 Clues You're a Girl Who's Heart-over-Head for Romance

1. You call radio stations to dedicate songs to guys you like so often that all the DJs know you by name.
2. You spend your free time baking cookies in the shape of letters so you can spell out the name of the guy you like.
3. Your cell phone bill is outrageous from texting the guy you've got a crush on.
4. You sing love songs in your head and stick your own name in the lyrics.
5. You've actually written a love note on some guy's car with lipstick.
6. You're now fluent in three languages, love skateboarding, took up art, and are into video games, all because the guy you like is too.

7. You've sent flowers, candy, or gifts to win the heart of a hottie.

8. When you and your boyfriend went for pizza, you had the pizza guy arrange all the pepperoni into the shape of a big heart.

9. You spend all your Facebook time on your crush's profile, looking at the pictures that have both of you in them.

10. You practice signing your first name with his last name.

Heart-over-Head

So what does it all mean? For heart-over-head girls, here's the diagnosis: you're quick to get crushes on guys. You probably put a lot of energy into getting guys to notice you, and you almost always hope guys fall for you in return.

WHAT'S GOOD ABOUT IT: EMOTION

Being in touch with the sensitive side of our minds is a blessing. In our twenty-first-century world, emotion is usually replaced with intellect. Our world is full of logic and science. And the world is down on just about everything that can't be proved through facts and figures.

A mind in touch with emotion is a welcome change. Sometimes it's a fresh perspective on the world to let our feelings guide us. A feeling like the spark we get when we're excited, falling in love, or just have a crush on a guy can tap into emotions that people often keep all bottled up inside. When girls are too afraid of letting their true feelings show, they can miss out on some of life's best experiences.

WHAT RISKS COME WITH IT: INFATUATION AND LUST

If you fall in love with every guy you end up having feelings for, your life will become a teenage soap opera. Before you know it, people will be calling you Blair and you'll think you live in Manhattan, caught between your cheating boy-friend, Nate, and Chuck, his best friend.

Soap opera–style relationships are on TV for a reason: they don't work in real life. When people get close to one another, it's not like they can just switch gears one episode later and fall for somebody else. If you're a heart-over-head kind of girl, you run this risk. Infatuation is short-term and usually ends up going nowhere. It fizzles out and you're left wondering what all the energy was for in the first place.

The second risk is lust. When infatuation goes too far, it's like your body takes over and your mind gets thrown in the backseat. This can lead to a girl making some pretty bad decisions. Going too far physically, or starting to compromise emotional or religious values that you care about can be the result of lust.

What God Says About It: Emotions Are a Gift . . .

But watch it when your emotions get the better of you. The Bible's full of places where we're encouraged to use our thoughts, our positive emotions, and our imaginations in ser-vice of the Lord.

The best example? The Psalms. Take one book, add a couple hundred chapters, throw in some old-school musi-cal instruments, and you get song after song that's filled with emotion.

The Psalms feature shout-outs to God, to lovers, bless-ings, friends, nature, animals, music, good health, harmony, good times, and about sixty-five zillion other things. The words aren't about highbrow intellectual thinking. The Psalms are about emotion. It's almost like you wonder if King David had any free time after getting all *American Idol* about it and leaping across the grounds of his palace while singing his heart out all day long.

Emotion has a downside, though. The best place to see the risks of emotion? Keep following the story of King David. His instant lust for Bathsheba led to a total mess in his life. He not only had sex with somebody else's wife, but he also had her husband murdered just to try to cover the whole thing up.

You may have heard this story a thousand times, but it's worth remembering. Emotion turned to lust usually ends up going bad. Like I said, the fire that you feel initially will eventually fizzle out, and you're the one left with the consequences: guilt, sorrow, shame, confusion, and a feeling that you and God aren't getting along or you're getting distant from him.

Big Myth: You've gotta start liking a lot of guys to ever find your true love.

Real Deal: You've gotta let yourself have feelings for guys, but you don't have to have a crush on every one you meet.

10 Clues You're a Girl Who's Head-over-Heart for Romance

1. You like to split the bill when you and a guy go out on a date.
2. You've never jumped into the car with a girlfriend and secretly stalked a guy you liked just to find out where he lived.
3. When you go to the beach, you actually wear a bathing suit that's functional, not for him to ogle at.
4. You've never pretended you weren't home when a guy called, just to make him anxious or want you more.
5. You're looking for friendship first, and then romance.
6. You know exactly what you're looking for in a guy and won't settle for less.
7. You don't have any stuffed animals named after guys you like. Not even one.

8. You're fine sporting two-day-old hair, no makeup, and mismatched clothes in front of him.
9. You say, "Bring it on!" to seconds if you're still hungry when you guys go out to dinner.
10. You don't care if your guy knows what size jeans you wear or how much you weigh.

Head-over-Heart

For head-over-heart girls, the situation's a bit different. You're all for even-stevens and equality. You're not going to have a massive crush after twenty minutes on a date, and you're looking for a sign that feelings between you two are mutual before you leap into anything major. But here's the downside diagnosis: all this equality means a lot of waiting around to see what develops over time. And as time goes on, you risk getting to know so much about a guy that makes him seem cool, you sometimes forget he might not have some of the main qualities you're looking for, like being a Christian, for example.

What's Good About It: Equality and Reciprocity

Reci-what? you ask. You may not use the word that often, but if you're a girl who usually falls head-over-heart when it comes to romance, you know all about it.

Reciprocity (ress-i-pross-i-tea) is an exchange. You know, like you give a little—I give a little. When girls are the head-over-heart type, they're looking for this kind of swap. They don't want to be the only one who has the crush. And they don't want to give up other stuff in their life that's fun, just to hang out with a guy. Instead, girls like this are all about give-and-take. It's sometimes called "guarding your heart." It's about protecting yourself, since the chances of you (as two high school students) not getting married are pretty high.

Giving a little on both sides isn't the same as holding back love unless you get something in return. It's more of an even-steven kind of deal. The feelings are there, but you're not going to go all in for some guy you just met, change all your hobbies, and give up other stuff you like to do in your life if he's not feeling it too.

Being a head-over-heart girl can be hard, though. When we first start thinking we might like a guy *that* way, many girls fall hard. Waiting to see what turns out if you two take it on the friends level first can be more than a lot of girls can stand. Here's where the head-over-heart girl hits her stride. She's into using her mind to stop, look, and think about what's going on before she gives her heart away.

WHAT RISKS COME WITH IT: MISMATCHING AND PLAYING HOUSE

We've got three main risks that come with being head-over-heart for a guy. They are mismatching, missionary dating, and playing house.

Mismatching. Have you ever heard the phrase "unequally yoked"? It means that two people who aren't in the same place spiritually end up together. This often happens because one person is trying to "missionary date" the other—to save them and bring them to Christ.

But here's the real deal: you're a Christian girl. This means that you give it your best to follow God each day. It means you've got some ideas about what's what in the world today. And it means that you've probably got a clear idea about how you want to think about guys and sex.

If you end up with a guy who's not a Christian, you're ending up with a guy who might not share any of these ideas. So, the two of you end up being mismatched. Two things that don't really go together end up that way. He doesn't get the whole Christian thing. You don't get why he doesn't share your values.

Mismatching happens for a few reasons:

A head-over-heart girl is cool about guys, building friend-ships, and letting things develop over time, which means she's getting a clear idea of whom she's dating. The thing is, there are tons of guys who have amazing morals and lifestyles, even though they're not Christians. So, because a head-over-heart girl is able to hang with lots of different guys and see how amazing they are, she tends to forget that it's even important if these guys aren't believers. She figures that so much other stuff is good about a guy that it'll all work itself out in the end.

Learning how to work on equal footing with guys means we head-over-heart girls are able to put up with a lot. We can get along with almost anyone as long as they're down to do their part too. So if we end up getting close to a guy who's great at sharing, compromise, and being a teammate to us, we can forget one little thing: he's not a Christian. And what that means is that someday—maybe way down the road from right now—when you two try to be partners who follow God, you're going to run into trouble.

Missionary Dating. This is when a girl has a "burden" for a guy to bring him to Christ. This means dates, a serious relationship, and deeper levels of intimacy, all in the hope that someday, one day, just maybe even this day . . . he'll convert and come to God. But even a head-over-heart girl can't plan to make missionary dating work out just because it's been her plan all along. Take it from a girl who's been there: *God* is the only one who can call a guy to Christ—your kisses can't! Missionary dating doesn't always end up the way you'd like, and people don't always convert.

Dating a guy can bring growth to our lives. But don't forget that spiritual growth means you, your boyfriend, and God are all on the same page.

In the Bible, the big guy warning us against mismatching is Paul. In 2 Corinthians 6 he tells us that if we want to follow God, it's easier to do it with another person who wants to follow God too. His master plan for this to work out is: date people you know are going to be down with your religious beliefs. Date people who will help you grow and stay on track to become spiritually mature as you grow into womanhood.

"Okay, but it's not like I'm getting married tomorrow," you say. "Marriage is way off in my life, so what's the big deal?"

The big deal is that when we're getting romantic with guys, we're getting intimate on all sorts of levels. Sure, you may not run off to Las Vegas and have a quickie-drive-through wedding with your current crush, but you're setting a precedent for the kind of guys you will date in the future when you are more serious. And you will also still have to deal with big-time stuff in your relationship.

Like what? Well, like what are you guys going to do when you go out? Is he into partying and you're not? Does he think it's no big deal to lie so you guys can spend more time in private? What about prayer? Is he into it, or are you going to have to put it on the back burner when you guys are together? Is he into getting physical, but you want to wait? What about church? Are you going to meet up with him after service or youth group is over? Or, are you going to start skipping out so you can hang with him and his friends?

See what I'm talking about with the whole mismatching thing? Even if you're not about to walk down the aisle with some guy, there's still a bunch of stuff that you two will be on different pages about. And even if you can get the pages all worked out, you're going to be reading two different books, so to speak. You'll be into the Bible, but what's he gonna be reading?

Big Myth: It's fine to date non-Christian guys since I'm not about to get married, or anything.

Real Deal: It's hard to date non-Christian guys since you're not going to be on the same page.

Playing House While We Wait and See. Even if they don't plan to, some girls end up living in mismatched relationships. Sometimes a girl will choose to weigh the option of mismatching against the option of breaking up with a guy she's been into for a long time. In the end, she decides that mismatching isn't that bad of a proposition by comparison. And when a girl grows into this kind of mind-set, she's basically saying yes to a wait-and-see relationship.

After high school, many of these wait-and-see relationships turn into living arrangements. "I'll just move in with my boyfriend for a while, so we can see where things are going," say some girls.

But if you think about it, what have these girls really committed to? A guy, or the idea of the guy becoming something he's not? Hopefully you picked the second answer. The wait-and-see approach basically commits you to an idea, not a person. You become serious about the idea that a guy can be what you want. So in the meantime—while you're waiting-to-see—you keep dating, set up house, live together, and see if things can't turn out like you'd like them to.

Playing house can lead to lots of drawn-out, blown-up endings. Head-over-heart girls who've been hanging in there for years can finally explode when their dreams don't work out. Guys who date head-over-heart girls can feel duped or lied to. They didn't know their girlfriend was waiting to see some kind of miraculous change, like a conversion to Christ.

Romance—But What Kind?

No matter if you're the heart-over-head or head-over-heart kind of girl, you'll eventually take the plunge. No, silly, not that plunge. But the smaller plunge—the one into guys and figuring out how you want to spend time with them. When it comes to girls, guys, and how they should get romantic, there's lots of confusion and even more opinions.

Some People Are Going the Courting Route

This whole deal got big when a guy named Joshua Harris wrote a book called *I Kissed Dating Goodbye*. Just a little bit out of high school, Harris tried giving his life to God without trying to throw girls into the mix. He combined two parts self-control, one part commitment to his promise, and came up with this: courtship.

The basic deal is that courtship replaces dating (thus the title). Courtship isn't a kind of dating; courtship is its own deal. It's like living with a different perspective on romance.

Courting is a pretty simple idea. Here's how it works: guys and girls get involved because they're looking to get married. That's it. That's just about the whole deal. Two people click, get a vibe going, and then set off to find out if there's any reason why a marriage wouldn't work out.

It's straight-up friendship first when it comes to courting. No making out, no getting down. Because courtship is all about finding a life partner, different stuff ends up being the focus of the relationship than when two people date. Courtship gives people a way to focus on the heart, head, soul, and mind of another person—not the bod (although that doesn't mean you're not going to notice a nice set of abs or a sparkling pair of eyes).

Once you know what's up with what's inside the person you're into, then the only other stage is marriage. There's really just one level to your relationship until you tie the knot: friendship and personal exploration.

Other People Are Going the Dating Route

Dating is way less intense than courtship, because it's more about temporary relationships. In fact, girls who date end up dropping a bombshell if they admit they're shopping for a husband. Can you say . . . breakup? That's just not what dating is for—at least not at first.

Dating is a trial run, or a test to see if people gel. The test might be successful, or it might not. There's no way to tell except to give it a go. And there's usually no pressure for the relationship to go anywhere serious at first.

Dating is casual and can be broken off in a jiffy. But while it lasts, people usually move beyond friendship and into physical intimacy while finding out more about the other person. Both things usually go on at once: friendship and physical intimacy.

SOME PEOPLE AREN'T ON ANY ROUTE—THEY JUST LIKE TO FLIRT AND HANG OUT

Sometimes people who act this way are called "teases," "players," or "hustlers." They're the guys and the girls who just want to get you interested. They're not looking to get into a relationship, and they're definitely not looking for anything long-term.

This is a kind of confusing route, especially for teens. Why? Because girls (and guys) love to get attention. You're not a freak if you've ever gone out of your way to look great for a guy just to get him to notice you. You're not the only girl who's sat down next to a guy at a party and tried to act super-cute, funny, or witty to get him interested. Most girls have done it, even if they won't admit it.

But where does that stuff end up going? If you're not really interested in a guy, and you're flirting just to get attention, you're actually being kind of selfish. You're asking another person to give a part of himself to you. And if you ask for too much, you're asking for parts of that person's heart, mind, or soul.

When you hear about people who play "mind games," this is exactly what's going on. When someone needs attention, he or she tries to play with another person's mind and get it from them.

But don't think I'm going off on flirting here—I'm not. Flirting is totally natural. It's part of testing out what's going on with our developing sexuality. Just know that you can't let flirting get out of hand. It's not a way to get attention. And it may even lead to stuff that's hard to handle, like the pressure to have sex. Because you're using your body to get attention when you flirt, it's hard for guys not to pick up signals that you're into them in a physical way.

Straight-Up Advice

Giving romance a try isn't the same as becoming lost in a swirl of emotions and excitement. And this is where the advice comes in: get your head on straight. Know what kind of romantic you are (heart-over-head or head-over-heart), and take it slow.

The biggest mistake girls make in their teenage years is getting all dramatic about romance. Girls can sometimes spend hours, days, and even weeks worrying about guys, crushes, and what to do about these feelings. Girls can freak out when guys they like come near. Or they can spend their free time fantasizing about what love would be like with different people. Needless to say, all this boy-crazy energy is energy that's being taken away from other things in your life, like sports, family, or most important, your spirituality and relationship with God.

So hold your horses, girl. You don't need to wear these feelings on your sleeve like they're going out of style. You've got plenty more where they come from, and your life is going to last, oh . . . about seventy, eighty, or even ninety years longer.

There's no rush to fall in love or get romantic. Truth be told from a girl who's older: people even get burned out on romance. After getting into so many relationships and getting so romantic about so many people, it's like you just reach a limit and have to take a break.

Knowing this when you're a teen is worthwhile. I'm not trying to convince you it won't totally bite when some guy you're crushing on turns you down or breaks your heart. But you know what? You will live to see another day. For real. Your life won't end. It will just be a bummer for a while.

But then, life will take a turn for the better. This is just how life is: it goes in cycles. So keep this idea of cycles with you in your head. Crushes will come, and crushes will go. Romance will bloom, and then it will fade. It's all about cycles.

Eventually a cycle will come where everything will just click. But it's nothing that you can force. So sit back, chill, and listen to God. Figure out if you're heading into romance with your heart or with your head. But most important, figure out if you're heading into romance on God's timetable. Check yourself to be sure you're not forcing a romance that's taking time away from God's plan for your life. The two will meet up eventually—God's plan and your man.

But until then, just give romance some time. It's not like your wedding day is coming up next week. Wait to find that cycle where everything seems to click and you feel comfortable and secure about what's going on.

Chapter 3

Prejudice and Perception

Okay, go ahead and try to fill in the following sentences with the word that fits in the blank. We're talking about prejudice here, so don't cop out and act like you don't have any answers. To get to the bottom of prejudice, it's important to confront the stuff we think inside. So go ahead and be honest here . . .

- African-Americans are good at _____.
- _____ are the worst drivers.
- People from _____ run 7-Eleven stores and gas stations.
- Guys who do ballet are _____.
- _____ all get As and are the best at school.
- Tall people play _____.

When you see people cruising toward you, how can you tell whether or not they're jocks? What about geeks, punks, Muslims, or homosexuals; how can you spot them?

If you can come up with answers to these questions, then you're just like the rest of us. Though you know it's wrong to judge a person by the outside, you still do. Sometimes you spot a few things about a person right off the bat and then immediately label him or her. *She's a prep. He's a Jew. They're white trash.*

Welcome to the world of prejudice. The reason I'm having

you check out what you think about is because it's the easiest way for us to see what's up with stereotypes. If you came up with answers for any of the questions above, then you know what a stereotype is. It's a way to sum up a whole group of people by what they do, what they look like, or what they're interested in.

Prejudice is all about opinion. It's something that's not about facts, and it ignores our individuality. Prejudice is an opinion you come to without looking at the real information. It's an ongoing problem in our society. And as the globe becomes a smaller place with things like the Internet and television, knowing where your head's at with prejudice can only help you out in the long run.

America is one of the most diverse nations on the planet. So, unless you stay in your own small town forever, chances are you're going to run into, work with, live near, or have friends who aren't like you. They may have a different color of skin. They may have a different religion. They may have a different amount of wealth—they could be much poorer or much wealthier than you are. But in the end, you'll have to figure out how to view these people as equals.

Just a Label?

Some people get beautiful faces; other people get all the brains. The whole idea of equality when it comes to our physical bodies or our personal qualities and skills just doesn't hold true. We're not all equal in those ways.

But we all are equal as human beings. We all get nervous, cry, laugh, dream, get angry, and want community with other people. All this stuff is part of human nature. It's just the way God made us.

That's what *equal* means when we get down to it. It means that underneath all the looks and abilities, people have the same value. They have bodies, hearts, minds, and souls, just like us. They are made by God. This is the first place to begin when trying to understand what prejudice is all about. We have to get it into our heads that we're God's creations, just like everybody else. We're all human beings, and in that way, we're all equal to one another.

When prejudice creeps into our minds, we forget that. Instead of seeing other people as human beings, just like us, we see the person as a label. Some labels are about race, while other labels are about how much money people make or what country they come from. Either way, the label doesn't describe the person inside. It's just a name that people use *without* knowing the person underneath.

How does this end up happening? Why are people prejudiced in the first place?

Back in the Day . . .

Prejudice goes way back in human history. Remember the story in the New Testament about the good Samaritan? It's in the book of Luke. It tells all about how only one out of three men stopped to help a guy who'd been robbed. A Jew, a Levite, and a Samaritan all have the chance to help the guy. Only the Samaritan helps out.

The big deal with prejudice in this story is that the one guy who helps is typically considered the scumbag of the bunch. In ancient times, Samaritans were the lowest of the low. So when Jesus told this story, people probably figured that it would have been the Jewish guy or the Levite who'd stop and help, not a dirty Samaritan.

But Jesus busts this bubble of prejudice. Jesus makes the Samaritan the hero of the story. The Samaritan isn't dirty at all. Instead, he's kind, generous, and helpful, just like you'd want someone to be.

Every generation that's lived has had to deal with people being mean, violent, rude, or aggressively opposed to some other group. History has given us Caucasians who've oppressed African-Americans (slavery), Germans—Nazis—who hated Jews (the Holocaust, or *shoah*), Americans afraid of Japanese (U.S. internment camps), and most recently, extremist Muslims attempting to destroy Americans (9/11). These are the most hard-core, heavy-hitting examples.

But we've also seen other examples. In America, Native Americans were often killed and beaten for practicing "witch-craft." African-Americans used to be segregated, lower-class citizens because of their skin color. Women didn't have the right to vote.

In all of these cases, from the Samaritan in the Bible to the victims of 9/11, we can learn about prejudice by getting to its source: stereotypes, misinformation, and fear.

Stereotypes

The thing is, stereotypes tend to stick around because they are generally true. For example, many people who are tall and like sports *do* end up playing basketball. Think about it . . . the hoop is up high. If you're tall, then you're already that much closer to scoring. Not that many girls who are 4'11" are going to gear up to head out for the b-ball team in the fall. It's just not realistic that a girl this short would make the team.

So a stereotype can be true, in part. But here's where stereotypes lead to prejudice: when you see only the stereotype, not the person. For example, one short girl tries out for the basketball team. She ends up getting cut. But instead of people saying, "Kellyn totally stunk up her tryout, and the coach cut her in like two minutes flat," people begin to say things like, "Short girls like Kellyn all bite at basketball. Duh! They're midgets!"

In general, people aren't able to use stereotypes without being prejudiced. In the example above, one short person wasn't able to make the basketball team. But before you knew it, all short people couldn't play ball, and on top of that they were midgets! So even if the people gossiping about Kellyn are using stereotypes (even one they think is true), it means they're boiling a whole person (or a group of people) down to one quality that's typical about them. In Kellyn's case: she's short; she's a midget. So in the end, you don't know anything about Kellyn as a person. All you know about her is the stereotype you've heard; you don't know the person at all.

Big Myth: Christians are better than other people.

Real Deal: Christians are called to treat everyone with respect and love.

What you can take away from a story like this is three things:

1. Stereotypes can never describe a whole group of people. Everybody is an individual. No one word can ever describe this kind of diversity.
2. Stereotypes are usually just half of the problem. The other half of the problem is prejudice. If you buy into the stereotype, the next step can be hate.
3. A mind-set that focuses on stereotypes and builds prejudices is going to be incapable of following Jesus' requests that we love one another the way he asks us to in 1 John 4:7.

Misinformation

Misinformation most often makes its way to us in two forms: gossip and media. Here's how each of these works and what you can do to be sure you're getting what's real out of the information you hear.

GOSSIP

Here's the Deal: You know what happens when a friend tells a friend something she heard from another friend? Yep. Gossip. And the truest thing about gossip is that most of it isn't true. Same goes for "misinformation" when it comes to prejudice.

Prejudiced gossip can take many forms. It can be gossip about dumb stuff, like what people eat or what they look like. Or it can be gossip about things that are really important in a person's life, like religion or family.

Basically, prejudiced gossip is just trash talk. It's the same kind of trash people say about each other when they're being catty and spreading rumors. But in this case, it's trash and rumors about a person that attack their race, gender, or religion.

HERE'S WHAT YOU CAN DO:

Speak Up. When you hear people dishing gossip, try to put a stop to it by changing the subject or by calling your friends on their chitchat.

Head Out. If you can't stop the gossip, get yourself out of there. Not only is trash talk not a productive way to spend your time; Christians are also called to try to keep their heads above this kind of stuff. It isn't always easy, but you've got to give it a shot if you want to keep prejudice out of your worldview.

Look Into It. If you hear prejudice, take a second to check it out. Use the Internet to find out what's what with different kinds of people. A good way to do this is to head over to the on-line site for a big newspaper. In the search box, enter some of the words you heard people gossiping about and then check out what you find. Here are some newspapers you can try:

Dallas Morning News http://www.dallasnews.com
Washington Post http://www.washingtonpost.com

New York Times   http://www.nytimes.com
Chicago Tribune   http://www.chicagotribune.com

Another way to look into prejudice is to look up the words in a dictionary that you hear people using. Find out what the real definitions are and what the words should mean when they're not part of prejudice.

MEDIA

Here's the Deal: Everybody knows there are a zillion opinions about stuff going on in the world, but not everything you read or see is the truth. People sometimes report facts and figures, but other times they report their opinions of these facts and figures, which can lead to something less than the truth. It can lead to misinformation.

This may sound a bit confusing, but you totally know what this looks like in real life. Here's an example:

Let's say that your friend bombs the weekly vocab test in English class. In fact, let's say almost everybody bombs the test. It was tough. Later that day you're at your locker and hear somebody talking about the test. When you tune your ear in to listen, you hear one girl say, "Yeah, I heard most people didn't score very high because the test was so hard."

But you also hear a girl chime in right after. She follows up on the comment and says, "The test was hard, but people failed because nobody studied."

Can you tell which girl was giving facts and figures and which girl was giving her opinion?

The fact of the matter is that the test was tough. That's a hard fact. If you wanted to check out the truth of the statement, you could. You could hunt down the teacher who made the test and ask if she intended it to be hard or not. She made it, so she's the source of the real-deal information.

But girl number two doesn't know whether anyone studied or not. So when she gave a reason why people failed the test, she was just guessing. And it's those kinds of guesses that you want to watch out for. They're what's called "misinformation." The information can be "mis"leading because there's no way to tell whether or not it's true.

Misinformation is stuff that's not definite fact. Instead, it's an opinion—a guess. Somebody hears a piece of information and then tries to figure out the who, what, why, where, and how details just by assuming or guessing. Wrong guesses can give you a completely different picture of the situation than might actually be true. And oftentimes, people assume that these guesses are truth. That's where you get misinformation.

Big Myth: Stereotyping people isn't a big deal.

Real Deal: Stereotyping people leads to prejudice.

HERE'S WHAT YOU CAN DO:

Be Wary. Don't go full-boat and believe everything you hear. It doesn't mean that you have to be suspicious that everyone is trying to lie to you. It just means to be cautious.

Learn to Identify Facts and Figures from Opinions. Remember, prejudice happens when we're *without* the real facts. If we're getting a big dose of opinion, we might be *without* the information we need to make a good decision that's free of prejudice.

Fear

We fear what we do not know. The phrase basically means that when we're faced with something new or foreign, it can freak us out. We don't know what's going on. We don't know how to act.

It's pretty normal for you to feel out of your element when you're around people who do stuff differently than you do. Most people hang with others who are just like them in a lot of ways. Think about your school, for example. Most of the cliques that hang out probably have a bunch of things in common. Some of these things might be hobbies, like playing sports, or being into band. But other things keep people together, too, like race or religion. Asian kids might hang out with other Asians, just like Christians might hang out with other Christians.

Why don't ethnic, racial, or religious groups mix more often? Sometimes the answer is fear. When we group with others who are like us in some way, we don't have to worry about too much. We know we'll be understood, and we won't be uncomfortable. When we move outside this group, fear and prejudice can kick in. Things are new and you're scared.

What do you do? Well, you've basically got two choices: stay afraid or be bold.

STAYING AFRAID

Prejudice usually results when people make the first choice: stay afraid. Instead of getting to know the new people around them as human beings, they close up. They rack their brains for reasons why they don't have to find out about the new people around them. They search for reasons why it's okay to stay away.

Wanna know the kind of excuses people sometimes come up with? Stereotypes and prejudice. It's like we use the bad things we've heard about a people group to make ourselves feel better that we didn't get to know them. We use these excuses to stay away.

In reality, though, we're just fearful. We don't understand all the new stuff around us. We're afraid that if we tried to make friends, we might be rejected. Or, we're just really stubborn and think that our way is the best way. We don't want to hear about anything that might prove us wrong. We're afraid of what we'll find.

Being Bold

If you choose the second option—be bold—you're choosing the option that will lead to a less-prejudiced view of the world around you. But being bold doesn't mean that you have to go out and get all fake about who your friends are. If you're a preppy girl, it doesn't mean you have to start sporting cornrows and listening to hip-hop. If you're a girl who has immigrated to the USA from another country, you don't have to give up your name and start calling yourself "Jennifer" or "Mary."

Being bold is something different. It's about looking at and listening to what's going on inside you, and looking at and listening to what's going on inside other people. You've got to give others the same space to have opinions, customs, or religious beliefs as you have.

Being bold is about forgetting your prejudiced assumptions and leaving judgment behind. It's about getting to the bottom of stuff you want to know by asking good questions and listening to what others have to say, not by assuming what you think is true about their life, beliefs, or behavior. It doesn't mean that you'll agree with their ideas all the time, but it does mean that you listen up and open your mind to consider what they're about.

And let's be honest, that's something we could all really use, right? To have people in our lives bold enough to actually take time to learn about us. To have people bold enough to try to understand what we're doing even if they don't agree.

Chapter 4

Pressure and the Real You

I'd like to tell you that I've always been a girl so sure of herself that I never paid one ounce of attention to peer pressure. That I was so secure in my identity that I never once was tempted to do anything I disagreed with. It would be great if that were the truth—especially for my parents. Oh, the horror they had to endure! When I embraced my teenage years of rebellion, my mama must have been down on her knees in prayer almost every night.

After all, my teenage rap sheet is longer than a double roll of Charmin: I egged houses. I took my parents' minivan out without their permission. I ditched school. I shoplifted with friends. I lied about things to get people to like me. I cheated on tests. I snuck out of the house. I lied about where I was going and whom I'd be with. I snuck into movies. I had a fake ID so I could get a tattoo. I toilet-papered neighborhoods. I ditched youth group. I tried pot. I stayed out past curfew. I snuck into amusement parks. And so on and so forth.

The good news is, my rebellion lasted all of about a year and a half. I never became a serious "problem child." The time I spent going wild was like something my friend told her parents when she got caught sneaking their car out for joy-rides. She said, "Mom . . . I don't really have a good excuse for taking off in the car. It's just . . . I just wanted to do something bad—something cool that I could tell other people about, you know?"

And that about sums it up for me too. I just wanted to try some stuff that was bad (or at least bad in that wanna-be-bad-like-a-kid-from-the-suburbs kind of way). It's not that I wanted to go punk or anything. I just wanted to push some limits. I wanted to do something that I thought was cool. I wanted to show myself that I was capable of breaking out on my own. If consequences came with it, then so what? I wanted to try it anyway.

This is where peer pressure stepped into the picture.

Peer pressure said, "Hello to you, my friend."

And I said to it, "Hey, aren't you . . ."

But, before I knew it I was running off with a crew of girls, having just ditched fifth period. That's how peer pressure can be sometimes: friendly, fun, and something that catches you up in an instant. But peer pressure can also turn out for the worst. It can be too much to bear. It can get us into trouble. And it can weigh down on us like a ton of bricks. It's like we're doing all we can to keep it off our back, but it never goes away.

The reason peer pressure is so powerful is because it's all about emotion. Peer pressure sneaks around our minds and peeks into what we're feeling. Do we wish we were cool? Are we totally bored? Can we even stand it that some other person got the grade we worked really hard for?

When our emotions are exposed like this, peer pressure knows it's time to move in—time to zoom into your head and ask, push, or talk you into doing something that you normally wouldn't, except now you've got some pretty intense feelings that are making you want to act.

Let me give you an example.

This one's about your boyfriend, and it's pretty standard. He wants to go all the way. You want to keep things the way they are. You're not into having sex, and you're fine being a virgin. On the other hand, he's into checking the whole sex thing out. He says you guys could just do it once, to see what it feels like. Then, if you don't like it, you can go back to the way things are now.

Let's also say that this guy's your first big-time boy-friend. He's the guy you've had a crush on for years and you've finally gotten together with him. It's been going all right, and you've been dating for almost six months now. You know he likes you, and you guys get along great. But he's really popular, and girls always talk about how cute he is. (Duh . . . that's why you had a crush on him in the first place, right?) He's hot, and you're a little bit tempted by his idea to try sex, just once.

You know for sure that some of the girls who have crushes on him have had sex before. It's not like he's going to ditch you for somebody else, but you just can't stop thinking about those other girls—they seem experienced, and you seem like a prude. So you've been talking about how his parents are going to be gone this weekend. On Saturday night they're going to his little brother's piano recital, and he'll have the house to himself.

He wants you to come over. You know what his invitation means. And even though you think he's kind of a jerk for put-ting you in an uncomfortable situation, you really like him.

What do you do?

Pent-Up Pressure

Just reading this made-up scenario might be enough to make you nervous. It's full of the kind of overpowering pressures that we girls go through in our teenage years. It's like we're being torn in too many directions to figure out how to make a good choice.

But let's break the story down and think about what you'd probably feel if you were put in that situation:

Pressure

The situation is challenging you. You're being asked to try and experience things you feel are wrong at this point. The feeling comes from people that are closest to you. You don't want to compromise what you believe in, but you also don't want to lose your friends—especially your boyfriend.

Anger

The situation is pushing your buttons. You're being asked to try things beyond your comfort zone. Because you're being pushed, you start to resent the person who's doing the asking.

Jealousy

The situation worries you. You feel like your boyfriend will like other girls more than you. You feel like you're not as good as somebody else. You're worried that you don't measure up. And even though you might not want to be like the people you're being compared to, you begin to wish you had what they have.

Lust

The situation gives you a craving. You might know the desire is wrong at this point in your relationship, but you just can't seem to stop the intense eagerness or enthusiasm that you feel inside.

Fear

The situation is nothing short of terrifying. Say yes, and you risk losing a part of yourself you really respect—your virginity. You risk getting your parents absolutely furious with you if they found out. And you risk getting pregnant or getting a disease.

Reviewing the list, we have six key emotions that go with feeling peer-pressured into doing something. It isn't just about feeling the weight of somebody asking us to do something we might not want to do; it's about a whole bunch of feelings at once.

Peer pressure works best when we've got all these emotions on our plate. Like I said, if we weren't dealing with this many feelings, we might be able to make a good decision with a clear head. But, because we're on an emotional roller coaster when it comes to peer pressure, we have a lot of breaking points.

Pressure Release

When we check out the roles that emotions and feelings play in our being peer-pressured, it's easy to see how peer pressure can overwhelm us. But dealing with peer pressure isn't just about saying no when these emotions hit us. It's also about learning to say, "What's up with my emotions?" when you begin to feel put upon by people or situations.

Try using a little guide like the one below and on the next page to jot down the emotions that are piling up on your plate the next time you feel pressured:

Into Our True Selves

Pressure during your teenage years comes in all shapes and sizes. You'll experience pressure to do or not do and like or not like all kinds of things in your life. From music to clothes to food to teachers and even other friends, pressure asks us to choose.

Argh!! Inside I feel like screaming at the people who are pressuring me!

What makes me mad is:

1. ....

2. ....

3. ....

But I also feel:

Jealous | Stressed | Tempted | Confused | Stereotyped
Anxious | Curious | Excited | Frustrated | Suspicious
Lucky | Naughty | Suffocated | Boxed-in | Overwhelmed

If I give in, I'll probably end up getting:

1. ....
2. ....
3. ....

If I give in, I'll probably end up losing:

1. ....
2. ....
3. ....

For most girls, the choices they make end up defining who they are and who they become. What they choose and what they're into say a lot about who they are on the inside. And with all these choices, it can be hard to figure out who we really want to be.

The good part, though, is that God gives us a few clues. His Scripture is the ultimate guidebook when it comes to making decisions. Plus, we've got different ethnic backgrounds, abilities, family lives, tastes, and preferences. To stay true to who you really are, it's important to check this stuff out from time to time. Here's what matters most about what's unique to you—hold on to it, and you'll always have your mind centered on your true self:

RACE

The globe features as many skin colors and ethnicities as anyone could imagine. Each is different from the other in some way, making race a part of your life that makes you unique.

Race can mean a lot of things in your life. Unfortunately, when people fail to understand something that's new or different to them, they can become angry and hateful toward it. This kind of hate and anger can lead to discrimination and prejudice.

But on the other side of the coin, race can also bring your life in touch with your heritage. Because your race is a part of you that's tied to history, you will find stories, pictures, legends, languages, and arts that are all a part of your past. You may not practice these traditions now, but the past is open for you to explore when you feel comfortable learning more about yourself.

You can also open the past to learn about others by looking into someone else's race. You can begin to see how we're all similar under God's design—how we all have love, family, hope, desire, and we all dare to dream for something amazing in our future.

AGE

No matter how girls are dressing today, the real you can't be any older than you actually are. The whole age thing has become so tricky in society today. Younger girls are trying to look older, show more skin, and look more mature. But on the other end you've got moms trying to rock skinny jeans (yikes!).

On top of this, you can thank plastic surgery for making age a completely irrelevant thing in our culture. Face-lifts, Botox, tummy tucks, and liposuction all scream, "I'm not fifty, I swear!"

But what's the big deal with being fifty, anyway? For that matter, what's the big deal with being fifteen? You only get one year to live and learn about yourself at each of these ages. That's it—just 365 days of being fifteen or fifty. So make the most of it! This is why it's important to embrace your age and use it wisely.

If you're older and always living in the past, where are you? If you're younger and always trying to live in the future, where are you?

You want the answer? You're nowhere. Here and now doesn't exist for you because you're pining away for the past or anticipating the years to come. The present is passing right before your eyes—and you're missing it!

HOBBIES

Inside your heart there are a couple of things that really get you going. For some people, it's music. For others, it's art, camping, singing, cars, literature, sports, computers, poetry, carpentry, or crafts. There's just no telling what will grab a girl's interest. But when something does, a wise girl listens up.

When you give up your time to hobbies, you're giving up your time to understand how you react, learn, and grow to things around you in the world. Because you're trying new things, you're allowing your soul to be creative and to make goals come true. Succeeding at these things can boost self-esteem. And when you look for your center as a woman, self-esteem is something you need.

Having hobbies means having a life that's rounded and whole. Because your true self is something created out of experiences, your hobbies provide a way to test yourself. You won't always succeed, but you won't always fail either. And the best part? Your passions are always there, no matter what the outcome. You can try again, or try something entirely new.

When you know what interests you, it's easy to find your true self. Getting involved in hobbies expands these interests and leads you to new parts of yourself that will develop as you grow.

Big Myth: Peer pressure is all about people making you do things you don't want to do.

Real Deal: Peer pressure is all about your emotions getting the better of you.

TASTES

The tastes we have are endless. We've got tastes in music. We've got tastes in foods. We've got tastes in fashion, makeup, hair, beauty, body, and guys. And we've got tastes in organizing, getting work done, and setting goals.

A girl's true self has a lot to do with her particular tastes. Tastes are like the speed that girls choose to live at each day. The things you pick, from the music you dig to the kind of mop you use to clean the floor, all have something to do with the kind of vibe you're trying to create for your life.

In your life, these choices create a space around you that's comfortable—an environment that's run the way you like. For example, you might like to create a space that's energetic, relaxed, cautious, organized, fun, or calm. And when you make choices that create these kinds of atmospheres, you're also learning about your comfort zones as a person.

Tastes that push you beyond the vibe you're used to experiencing might upset you. You can end up angry, frustrated, or stressed. That's why finding your true self is about listening. It's about hearing your mind communicating with your body to create the arrangement that's right for you.

TALENTS

Blessings come in many forms. That's the reason girls end up with different talents. Nobody gets it all, but most of us get a pretty good set of talents to work with.

For example, my sister and I both ended up being interested in artsy stuff. She's down with painting, drawing, and music. I'm down with writing, graphic design, and Web work. But guess what? Both of us missed the boat when it comes to coordination. Let's just say you don't want to get on a dance floor with either one of us unless you're ready to get thoroughly embarrassed (and potentially injured too!).

So we stink at the whole coordination deal. So what? It's kind of a bummer because we both like to dance, but our talents in other fields make up for it by a mile. And that's what finding your talent is all about—discovering things you're good at and interested in doing. The other stuff you're not so hot at will pale by comparison. Mixing what you like and what you're good at can lead to self-esteem, a sense of accomplishment, and a true sense of what you're capable of.

Talent can also help a girl find her center when it's put on display. Sure, knowing what you're good at can give you a sense of accomplishment, but what about showing off your stuff? Using and showing off your talent on a regular basis gets you in the habit of remembering what you're good at. It's a way to remind yourself that you've got a creative side that's yours to express. During your teen years, knowing this can be a blessing. With all the worry over who looks like what and how popular so-and-so is, your talent is a refuge. Your talent goes deeper and defines a part of who you are. You may even feel that it is what God has made you to do.

CULTURE

My parents aren't emigrants from another country. They've lived in America all of their lives, and so have my grandparents. And though I've got somebody way back there who came to the United States from a different culture, by this time it's long gone in my family.

Or is it? Culture is hard to define because most people think that you've got to be from a foreign country to have it.

But I'm going to beg to differ here. There's no use in thinking that just because most people around you look and act like you do, you've got no culture. It's just not true. The real you is part of a long history of culture. It just might not seem that way until you open your eyes.

Culture is made up of the arts, beliefs, actions, traditions, and products that people who live in community share and produce. That means whether you come from another country or not, you've got culture in you. You've got a group of people around you who have their own way of doing things and thinking about life. And if you were raised around these ideas, you've got yourself some culture, girl. You may just need to figure out what it is.

Culture can help you find your real self when the world gets too complex. The traditions or patterns of your family can be a safe place to relax and find support. Opening your eyes to discover the roles people play in your community and the ideas people hold dear can teach you about others. These roles and ideas will also teach you about yourself—about how far you've come, what you'd like to change, and what you want to be sure you focus on as you grow into womanhood.

Big Myth: Christians have to be prejudiced against people from other religions.

Real Deal: Christians have to respect people, no matter what their religion is.

RELIGION

Last, and most important, is God. You may not think it's any big deal every week when you get up and go to church. But being involved in a religion is a major part of who you are. Your beliefs, morals, dreams, goals, standards, and style of life have all been shaped because of your religion.

Religion is a choice. You decide to stop and pray. You let God be a part of your life. You decide to make time to study the Word. You take chances and head out on mission trips. And you get out and involved with your church community.

All of these choices will impact who you are. And each time you make any choice that's related to your religion, you're shaping a part of your true self.

This can lead to religion's having a big impact on who you become as you grow into womanhood. Because you choose to follow a particular path now, you will end up at a particular location later. Everything is connected to religion.

Because of this connection, finding your real self has a lot to do with taking the time to be sure you're committed to something you care about—not something you're doing just because your parents told you to. Religion is something that asks for your body, mind, and soul. If you give this away, then you've given your life to something that makes you distinct. You've committed your life to God, whom you'll try to honor as you make your way through life.

Not everyone gives themselves in this way. So don't kid yourself about the role faith plays in finding your true self. It's something you've got to choose for yourself if you want it to be something where you can find your real center.

Chapter 5

Going Online and the Digital You

Katie Meier is writing a book! Look familiar? Your news feed on Facebook is probably full of status updates like this—little tidbits and funny posts from all your friends.

We're all totally plugged into the digital and electronic world these days. Think about how often you check your e-mail, your profile, and your phone. Instant access is always just a few clicks away, which, like most things, has its positives and negatives. It's actually really cool that we can connect and stay in touch so easily; it opens up so many opportunities for friendship and fellowship.

And have you noticed how much easier it is to talk to guys online? So not as awkward as in real life. That little boost of confidence is a good thing, but it's also the biggest problem with electronic communication. It's super easy to become someone else online and do or say things you never would in real life, which is why we need to figure out the Digital You.

When you pick out the clothes you're going to wear, you're deciding how you're going to present yourself to the world. It's the same thing in digital. Everything you type, whether it's on a computer or a phone, says something about who you are. Maybe you text with everything abbreviated, like "R u comin 2mo?" or maybe you spell it all out, like "We're heading over to Christie's tomorrow. Do you want to come along?" That's such a small little detail, but it *does* change the way you come across.

So let's do it. Let's figure out how the digital you matches up with the real you. R u ready?

Texting

When were you allowed to get your own cell phone? Middle school? That's pretty much the norm right now. Having your own cell makes things really convenient when your parents need to pick you up from dance class or basketball practice or whatever. (Remember the days of getting left behind? You can kiss those good-bye!) Having a phone also opens up a whole new way to be social with your friends, and one of those ways is texting.

Self-Awareness

Just like the real you has to remember to live in the moment, the same goes for the digital you. It's really easy to get caught up in text convos with your friends and forget that you're sitting in a room with people. Even when we don't mean to be, we can be rude about our phone habits. Being self-aware helps with that.

When you're talking to your family or to people at church or others you respect, put the phone away. They'll appreciate having your undivided attention instead of you typing away while they're trying to talk to you. And yeah, it may cramp your social style a little bit, but it's worth just excusing yourself from the group for a moment if you want to respond to a message or answer a call. So not a big deal, but it's the small things like that that people notice.

Tone

The toughest part about texting (or any electronic chat) is that it's really hard to communicate tone. That's why people end up using all the smileys :) and the exclamation points!!!!!

Did you know that more than 90 percent of human communication is nonverbal? That means that we learn and understand more about each other through body language, facial expression, and tone of voice. So with texting, we have to operate in that tiny little 10 percent, which can be really hard.

Here's an example: Heather texts her friend Sara to ask whether she should wear her new green top to the dance on Friday, and whether she's *sure* she looks good in it. Sara laughs when she reads it because Heather looked awesome in that shirt when she tried it on. So she replies and says, "yeah haha, cuz ur such a fatty."

Obviously this totally depends on the person and the relationship, but it's not hard to see how Heather might not get that Sara is joking and therefore get upset about this. Humor, even good-humored teasing, is almost impossible to communicate by text. It can cause a lot of drama if you accidentally offend someone over text because you're not even there to see that she's upset! It might take hours before another friend tells you about it, and by then the whole thing has been blown way out of proportion.

Big Myth: Texting makes it really easy to communicate.

Real Deal: Texting makes it really easy to *mis*communicate.

So what can you do about it? Always hit Pause before you hit Send. Take just a second to read over what you've written before it goes out. It'll be pretty obvious if it's something someone could take the wrong way. Edit and then send. Even if it's a less interesting message, less funny or clever, it's worth it to avoid the potential blow-up.

Chances are you're going to be on the receiving end of an unfortunate text at some point, so you should be prepared for that too. Never text back when you're upset or angry. You will always say something that you'll regret. (Trust me. Been there, done that. Bought the T-shirt.) The best thing to do when you get a text that is upsetting is to approach the sender in person and ask her to explain what she meant by it. Potentially emotional conversations (breakups, arguments, etc.) should happen in real life, not digital life. It's much harder and makes us feel really vulnerable, but it's so much better for us. It helps us grow into self-assured women who don't have to hide behind an electronic screen when we have something to say.

Sexting

Texting back and forth with a guy you're crushing on can be really, really exciting. You hear that phone beep and your heart starts beating fast and you feel all fluttery as you open the message. What did he say? *He wrote back so fast; he must've been waiting for my reply,* you're thinking. Some of the best messages you'll ever get will be after a date, when he texts just to say how amazing you are and how he can't wait to see you again. Texts can make you feel super warm and fuzzy, which is why girls just can't get enough.

So what happens when the warm and fuzzies become something else? Here's what I'm talking about:

GUY: So what r u doin 2nite

YOU: Mmm, think i'm goin 2bed early. Long day w rehearsal!

GUY: Aww. Ur hangin in your pjs? Lol Sounds fun.

YOU: Oh it is. Can't wait!

GUY: btw i think Mark's party is gonna b lame anyway. Wish i cud join u instead ;o)

YOU: Well its pretty boring. sumtimes u just need to b antisocial tho

GUY: really? i think itd be pretty fun 2b in ur bed ;oP i really wanted 2kiss u @tom's btw.

YOU: Uh, really?!

GUY: yeah. u wanna hear what else id like to do w u?

Suddenly you're swept up in something you never intended to get into. Welcome to the world of sexting, ladies. It feels dangerous, which can be exciting, but it will end in disaster.

In addition to texting words, now we can send pictures over our phones. This is great if you just got a really cute puppy and you want to show your boyfriend. This is not great if your boyfriend is trying to get you to send suggestive pictures of yourself to him. Never, ever, ever take or send nude or semi-nude pictures of yourself or anyone else. If someone sends one to you, delete it! Once you send a picture of yourself, you have no control of it. It can end up in the locker room, at the party, and worst of all, on the World Wide Web. Do you know how many creepy men are on the World Wide Web? A lot.

Sexting has caused arrests due to images of minors being released, and even suicide because of the stress, shame, and ridicule from sexting nude images. Keep your clothes on and your camera phone focused on the dog.

If someone has started pressuring you about sexting, there are a lot of things to think about. Here are just five to start:

1. Texts are saved on his phone. He could show anyone!
2. Is he actually alone while he's texting you? Or is he hanging with his buddies, who are egging him on?
3. Is he the one texting? Or did his friend take his phone?
4. Is this the kind of guy you should be into in the first place?
5. Are you being true to yourself?

The answer to that last one is probably a big ol' NO. If you text things that you wouldn't say in real life, then you are definitely not being true to yourself. The important thing to remember is that when a guy crosses the line, you can always just not respond. You don't owe him anything. If he's being suggestive and it's making you uncomfortable, don't reply. Cut him off. This will put you back in control of the situation, which will make you feel a whole lot better.

You should also have the confidence to write back or confront him in person to say that he's made you uncomfortable (and probably owes you an apology!) and draw the line. If you create the rules for yourself and for him, you won't have to worry about getting into some potentially impure and embarrassing situations.

Social Networks

Facebook, MySpace, and Twitter give you a voice on the Internet. It's kind of a power trip actually. You're allowed to get up on your own personal soapbox and shout to the world what you think, feel, and know. And you go, girl! You should feel totally free to do that. You also get to check out what's up and coming—the hottest movie releases, fashion, news—and find people who want to chat about it.

Much of what you do online is completely harmless, but there's always the potential for trouble. Not to freak you out here, but I'm sure you've heard about crazy online stalkers, inappropriate photos traveling far and wide, or even just the nasty comment that broke up a relationship.

Here's the general rule of thumb for all this stuff: never post anything you wouldn't want your grandpa to see. That's right, your very sweet, very protective grandpa. This goes for your profile info, your posts/tweets, your music player, and especially your photos.

Privacy

Facebook, MySpace, and Twitter all offer adjustable privacy settings. Facebook lets you decide who can see what for practically everything, MySpace allows you to limit your photos, whether people can post freely or have to submit for comment approval, and Twitter tweets can be made private for anyone you haven't approved as a follower.

Obviously it's entirely up to you what you want to keep to yourself and what you want to make available to the world. (And trust me, it really is available to the world unless you change the settings.) It's always recommended to keep your photos, your address, and your phone number private for safety's sake. If you don't know how to change these settings, just go to the Help function that's available on all three sites, or Google the answer.

However you decide to set up your account or profile, here are some other things to keep in mind:

Posts

Beyond the whole safety thing and the fact that a lot of the stuff you post can show up in search engine results (like on Google or Yahoo), everything you say on social network sites can have an effect on the people around you.

Even if you've got everything set so only your Facebook friends can see your profile and your posts, if you comment on a friend's photo, that comment will show up on the news feed of all her friends and all your friends. (Note: You can actually change the news feed settings, too, but if anyone comes across that photo, they'll still be able to see the comment.)

Why does this matter? The same reason a text message that comes off the wrong way matters. But this time it's public, which means there's the potential for public humiliation. Be considerate to others, and don't open yourself up to inappropriate comments either. If you remember to think about what effect you can have on the real world, you'll always be a loyal friend on Facebook, just like you are in life.

Profile

Whether it's the music or the background on your MySpace page, or the Interests you put on your Facebook profile, personal info can be a little tricky when it comes to this online stuff.

Okay, so you really like that new song that has a few words bleeped out on the radio . . . why not post it on your profile? It's harmless, right? Well, by itself, sure. This is not the end of the world as we know it. But what if you also mention that you're a dancer and you're working on your flexibility? That might be true, too, but you can see how that can come off as a little suggestive, right?

Big Myth: It's so much easier to be myself online.

Real Deal: It's so much easier to invent a new self online.

Add just a few things like this together and you've created the wrong impression. How do you avoid this?

Imagine that your profile didn't have a name on it but was totally anonymous. Now imagine that your best friend was reading it. Would she be able to tell who it was? Is it true to who you are in real life?

Or how about pretending that your profile belongs to a stranger? If it sounds like the kind of together girl you want to be, then you're doing a great job! If it doesn't, then start editing, girl. Often it just takes a few tweaks here and there to get everything back on track.

Pictures

Pictures are probably the most fun and the most sketchy

part of social network sites. I spend most of my Facebook time looking through all the photos. Hours of entertainment! Just like everything else I've talked about in this chapter, this is about taking a step back for a sec because, like they say, a picture is worth a thousand words.

The short version? Don't post goofy or suggestive photos of yourself or others. You deserve so much better, and if you keep up your end of the bargain with albums you put up, then chances are your friends will do the same.

Gossip Girl

Digital information can spread like wildfire! Maybe you've already experienced this for yourself. Someone tags you in a really stupid photo, but a ton of people have already seen it by the time you get around to detagging. Or maybe the nightmare situation occurs, and it gets e-mailed around to all your friends. Yikes!

What can you do?

Don't panic. This stuff goes away eventually. If you're comfortable, talk to the person who posted the photo and explain why it wasn't cool. Otherwise, it's all about taking charge of your own stuff. The next time something like that happens to someone else, don't participate. Don't forward the message or "Like" the post. It can be tough, but taking a stand is awesome.

Being true to yourself is tough, especially online. The repercussions and reactions can be totally out of whack when you least expect it. The most important part of all of this is just being aware of how easily miscommunications can happen. Whenever there's a screen or a keyboard between you and the person or people you're chatting with, the potential is there.

When you're being the Digital You, don't forget the person that really matters—the Real You. She's who this is all about, so protect her in every way you can! Now, get chatting, girl!

Chapter 6

Disorders and Who Can Help

This chapter isn't going to pull any punches. We're going to head straight into the disorders that can end up in a girl's life. Why? Because it's not worth getting all fake or chatty about this stuff. It's real. It's a big deal. And girls shouldn't be ashamed if they're going through it.

The fact is that eight million (million...not hundred, not thousand, not hundred thousand) people in the United States struggle with eating disorders. Want to know what percent of these people are girls? The answer is 90 percent. Almost all of them.

So in this chapter we're going to run down what a disorder is, what it looks like, what it can do to your body, and how you can speak up and get some help. Take this stuff seriously, ladies. Disorders can crush your body, mind, and soul if you don't admit you're suffering and get some help.

You're worth too much to be ignored. Read up and get yourself ready to understand why disorders are such a common thing for girls. Get ready to learn, but also get ready to see what you can do about it.

Eating Disorders

Most people get psyched to eat. It's something they look forward to. An ice-cream sundae is a treat. A cheeseburger and fries can be the best in late-night snacking. But for a girl with an eating disorder, food is the worst. A meal means another time in the day where she has to stress about food and/or find a way to hide her problem.

Before we get into the two biggest eating disorders that girls end up developing, you've gotta know this: eating disorders are serious business because they don't *seem* serious at all.

For example, your friend might start saying no to certain foods when you're together. Or maybe someone you know starts to excuse herself to the rest room after eating, returning to the table with watery eyes or a reddened face or neck. All this stuff could be an indication of nothing. Your friend might be passing on the snacks because she doesn't feel well, or she's full. And not everyone who needs to use the bathroom after eating should automatically cause your brain to send up little red flags that say, "bulimic!"

It's a tough call sometimes. The subtlety of an eating disorder is exactly what makes it difficult to identify, and even harder to get help for. Everything will *seem* fine. But here's a list of why what *seems* okay might not be okay at all.

First

Most eating disorders look really normal. You can't tell just by the way they walk or talk. You can't point them out, and they're not wearing a shirt that says, "Princess 0 Pounds." In fact, they do the same stuff everybody else is doing.

For example, pigging out is something almost every crew of girls gets together and does from time to time. But for bulimics, this behavior becomes something called *binge eating*, or just *bingeing*. A girl will eat a large quantity of food only to intentionally throw it up later. The same problem can happen with girls who suffer from anorexia. Though it's normal to exercise, girls who have an eating disorder might skip meals, eat very little, and then exercise constantly to burn away the calories they've eaten, plus more.

We can see from these examples how tough it can be to know if anything is wrong. Normal, healthy behaviors are often the very same things that girls who suffer from eating disorders do. It's hard to distinguish.

Second

Girls are secretive. We've got secret note-passing systems. We've got diaries and journals we hide from our parents and friends. And we've got sassy online screen names to use so we can IM people in disguise. In general, we gals have some pretty great secret-keeping skills. So when it comes to eating disorders, most girls keep this private, too . . . even from their best friends or their family.

For example, you might suspect someone you know has an eating disorder. But when you try to talk with her about it, she totally tries to shrug you off. Because eating disorders are very painful, many girls are ashamed of their problem. They don't know how to ask for help. It's not unusual for a girl to act like she's fine while putting a lot of effort into keeping her eating disorder a secret.

Third

Disorder is a dirty word. It sounds pretty serious. It doesn't sound like the kind of thing that would describe me if I liked to check my weight several times per day. It doesn't sound like the kind of thing that would describe me if I spent the day bummed out after finding that my favorite jeans didn't fit anymore. And it doesn't sound like the kind of word that would describe me just because I keep track of all the calories and fat I eat every day.

So if we say that we have—or someone we know has—a *disorder*, it sounds like we're saying something big is wrong. But it doesn't seem that way to us. The way we think about food *seems* pretty normal. To us, it's just our regular routine. Sure, we watch what we eat, but it's not like . . . a *disorder*, you know?

Big Myth: Skipping meals will help me lose weight.

Real Deal: Skipping meals to lose weight is a sign of an eating disorder.

But while nothing seems wrong, what might be happening is this: you, or your friend, are starting to become obsessive about particular foods or eating habits. Being obsessive means paying extra-careful attention to something, doing it over and over again all day long, and lacking the ability to knock it off, even if you try. Issues with body image and food can start small. This is sometimes called "disordered eating." The problem is that disordered eating often leads to a full-blown eating disorder.

An example of this might be a friend who eats super-small portions of food, but always has to say something like "Oh my gosh! I'm soooo bad for eating this!" She scolds herself over and over again when she eats. It's kind of in a joking way, but it happens almost all the time, even when she hardly eats a thing.

So it's tricky. The way a girl behaves around food could be totally normal. But these normal behaviors are part of an illness when a girl does them obsessively, or is unable to stop doing them even if she tries. It might not seem like a big difference between the two, but it is. And *disorder* is the right word for it.

Disorders Girls Have

On the next few pages you're going to find a list of disorders. Each disorder has a little checklist of things people do or say that usually indicate they're sick and could really use some good, loving help. Also, each disorder features a checklist of things other people might be noticing about you if you're sick and could use help.

Some girls have these disorders right now. Other girls are on their way to having a disorder because they do some of the things you'll find on each list but maybe not all of them, or they don't do them to a really intense degree. But if you notice that a lot of your (or your friends') habits are included on one of these lists, don't turn the page! Don't pass it off as "no big deal." Instead, get with somebody older who's cool, whom you trust, and have that person check out the list with you to determine whether or not you could use some help. Not every girl who does one of the things on these lists is going to develop an eating disorder. But they might.

Anorexia Nervosa

Other Girls That Do It: The Anorexia Nervosa and Related Eating Disorders (ANRED) organization reports that 1 in 100 girls who are between ten and twenty years old are starving themselves.

Girls Say It's Because:
- "I'm getting skinny."
- "I'm in control of my own body."
- "I'm making everything the way it should be."
- "I say what goes."

Other People Notice That I:
- skip all or part of meals.
- have started to grow soft, white hair on my face and neck.
- want to work out all the time.
- cut up my food into tiny bites and push it around my plate a lot.
- have lots of food rituals, like chewing a certain number of times before I swallow.
- have lots of rules about what I allow and don't allow myself to eat.

I Don't Tell Because:
- it's not that big of a deal, and I can handle it.
- I don't want to make anyone mad.
- I don't want to look stupid, like I made a mistake.
- everything is almost perfect, and I don't want to stop short of my goals.
- other people don't need to know what goes on in my life.

Where Help Is When I Need It:
- Anorexia Nervosa and Associated Eating Disorders (ANAD); online at: http://www.anad.org
- National Eating Disorders Association (NEDA): 1-800-931-2237 or online at http://www .nationaleatingdisorders.org
- Eating Disorder Referral and Information Center; online at: http://www.edreferral.com/

Bulimia Nervosa

Other Girls That Do It: ANAD reports that 4 in 100 girls who are college-age suffer from bulimia. For teens, the number is tough to calculate because teens that are anorexic can also be bulimic or develop bulimia later on.

Girls Say It's Because:
- "I have my own secrets."
- "I can control the way my body looks."
- "I can relieve my stress."
- "I'm making everything the way it should be."
- "I say what goes."

Other People Notice That I:
- seem really normal.
- excuse myself to the rest room after eating.
- take a lot of pills (like laxatives).
- have binges where I eat a ton, or exercise a ton.

I Don't Tell Because:
- it's not that big of a deal, and I can handle it.
- I don't want people to know I'm thin because I'm bulimic.
- everything is almost perfect, and I don't want to stop short of my goals.
- other people don't need to know what goes on in my life.
- I'm ashamed of the fact that I make myself throw up.

Where Help Is When I Need It: See the help offered for anorexia on the previous page. Centers that treat girls who are anorexic also treat girls who are bulimic.

Mental Disorders

When you get sick it's usually something that's here today, gone tomorrow, like when you get the flu or a cold. It's not that big of a deal, and you're up on your feet again in no time.

Mental illness is a lot like this, except you don't bounce right back. Girls can end up having problems that last years instead of just a few days or weeks. And what makes the situation worse is that sometimes you can't even tell a girl is sick.

Many mental disorders are just like eating disorders: nothing *seems* wrong. A girl who is depressed might feel bummed out inside but put on a happy face for everyone who sees her. If so, nothing seems like it's off when people hang with her. They think she's fine, but she knows she's a mess.

This is another way mental disorders can be just like eating disorders: they're private. It can be tough to make your friends come clean if you suspect they're struggling. And, it can be hard for you to admit you have a problem if you're the one who is suffering.

Because mental disorders can last for such a long time in

your life, the longer they linger in your head, the worse you get. You can lose the love you have for yourself as a person. You can lose your ability to dream, get inspired, or feel the power of God in your life. You can lose faith in your abilities, and you can lose touch with the people who are closest to you.

None of this is worth it. But this is something that's hard to realize if you're already suffering from depression, addiction, or a form of self-injury, like cutting. It can be difficult if you're already dealing with a mental disorder to say, "Nope, I'm done with that!" and just walk away.

Instead of thinking about mental disorders as something you should just up and quit one day in your life, let's take it a little slower.

Here are some common kinds of disorders. Let's read through the descriptions and see if anything rings true for you. If so, take the next step and use the resources to reach out. You're worth it.

DEPRESSION

Other Girls That Have It: The American Academy of Child and Adolescent Psychiatry reports that depression is something that happens to many people. About 5 percent of children and adolescents deal with depression, and many adults do too.

GIRLS SAY IT'S BECAUSE:
- "I can't function anymore."
- "I don't really care about anything."
- "I never feel like getting up, going out, or doing stuff."
- "I'm sad but don't know why."

Other People Notice That I:
- withdraw from my friends and spend time alone.
- get sad really easily, and even cry a lot.
- am moody.
- sleep or eat a lot.

I Don't Tell Because:
- I can't figure out what's wrong.
- I'm too tired to make a big deal out of it.
- nobody would do anything, anyway.

Where Help Is When I Need It:
- Meier Christian Clinics: 1-888-7-CLINIC; online at: http://www.meierclinics.com
- Depression and Bipolar Support Alliance: 1-800-826-3632; online at: http://www.dbsalliance.org

Cutting (or Self-Mutilation)

Other Girls That Do It: Cutting isn't a small-time disorder. Rutgers University's Network for Family Life Education puts the number of people who self-injure near two million. Half or more of these people are girls.

Girls Say It's Because:
- "I can't get my feelings out."
- "It's my private secret."
- "There's too much pressure in my life."
- "I can relieve all my stress."

Other People Notice That I:
- can't really talk about my feelings.
- started wearing long-sleeved shirts and pants, even when it's hot outside.
- am moody and get angry a lot.
- can't cope with things very well.

I Don't Tell Because:
- I deserve what I do to myself.
- people would think what I do is gross.
- I need the release.

Where Help Is When I Need It:
- Self-Abuse Finally Ends (S.A.F.E.): 1-800-DONT-CUT; online at http://www.selfinjury.com

SUICIDE

Other Girls That Do It: The *Journal of the American Medical Association* (*JAMA*) featured an article saying suicide was the third most likely cause of death for people ages fifteen to twenty-four. The same article said that even though boys end up killing themselves more often than girls, girls *attempt* or *try to* commit suicide far more often than boys do.

GIRLS SAY IT'S BECAUSE:
- "Things are hopeless."
- "I can control the situation."
- "Nobody cares about me, anyway."
- "People would be better off if I were dead."

Other People Notice That I:
- have big mood swings.
- withdraw from my friends and spend time alone.
- criticize myself a lot.
- have started talking about death and dying.

I Don't Tell Because:
- I figure nobody really cares.
- I'm not worth the trouble.
- nobody would do anything, anyway.

Where Help Is When I Need It:
- The National Strategy for Suicide Prevention: 1-800-273-TALK; online at: http://www.mentalhealth.org/suicideprevention

Addiction (Cigarettes, Alcohol, and Drugs)

Other Girls That Have It: In 2003, the Center on Addiction and Substance Abuse reported that girls are now equal to guys when it comes to being addicted to drugs and/or alcohol. But unlike guys, girls become addicted earlier in their lives. Also, girls who are addicted to cigarettes, alcohol, and drugs become ill more easily and more often.

Girls Say It's Because:

- "I'm just having fun; it's not that big of a deal."
- "Everybody experiments with stuff when they're my age."
- "I'm not addicted because I'll quit later on."
- "It makes me look cool, like an adult."

Other People Notice That I:

- have trouble focusing or concentrating.
- burn through lots of extra money.
- have new friends that seem shady or older.
- have bloodshot or sleepy/lazy-looking eyes that are glazed over.
- smell like cigarette smoke or liquor, even though I've put a lot of perfume or cologne on.

I Don't Tell Because:

- I don't have a problem.
- It's not a big deal.
- I'm planning to quit.
- I don't want anyone to know.
- I can't stop because I owe people.

Where Help Is When I Need It:

- The Center on Addiction and Substance Abuse: Teens; online at: http://www.casacolumbia.org
- D.A.R.E. Kids; online at: http://www.dare.com

Getting Help and Getting Yourself Back

The most frustrating thing about being depressed, wanting to kill yourself, being addicted, or hurting yourself by cutting is that the real you gets lost.

Big Myth: Mental illness is just like being sick: it will go away eventually.

Real Deal: Mental illness is a form of sickness, but it can last forever if you don't reach out for help.

It's an absolutely frustrating cycle when girls get caught in it. And the only way out of the cycle is to speak up. Here's a list of places and people who can give us their ear when we've got problems.

Start at any of these points to get help. You'll be on the way to turning off the switch forever and keeping hold of the real you.

	Parents	Support Agencies	Psychologists	Psychiatrists
Who are they?	You know them better as Mom and Dad. But your "parent" could also be an aunt, uncle, grandma, or other relative.	Groups of people who run clinics or support centers, just because they want to help.	People who went to college to study how our minds work. They specialize in helping people understand what the deal is inside their heads.	People who went to medical school and became doctors (MDs).

	Parents	Support Agencies	Psychologists	Psychiatrists
Why can they help?	These people know you, but more important, they love you. Parents don't want to see their children hurting.	Support agencies specialize in different problems. You can find a support agency that's got the 411 on just the problem you're having.	Psychologists study the way people's brains work. They've spent tons of time talking to people with problems and are specifically trained to help people with mental disorders.	Psychiatrists go to medical school. This means they can check out both your body and your mind to see what's going on. They can also prescribe medicine for illnesses.
How do I get them to listen?	Parents can sometimes miss all the signs that you're crying for help inside. If you need a parent to be there for you, it's best to find some time alone with them and just speak up.	Support agencies can't find you; you have to speak up and go to them. Read up online; then call their hotline or phone number to get connected with someone who'll listen.	A psychologist might be working at your school. If so, you can e-mail them or stop by their office. If you don't have a psychologist at school, then you'll have to go to one's office to get help.	Because a psychiatrist is a medical doctor, you have to schedule an appointment to see one. In some states your parents will have to do this for you.

	Parents	Support Agencies	Psychologists	Psychiatrists
Who's going to find out about it?	Just your parents!	A support agency might contact your parents, another group, doctor, or counselor in your area if they need to know.	A school counselor will record the fact that you visited, but what you tell the counselor is private. If you see a psychologist that your parents arrange for you to see, they can speak to your parents about what they hear in some states.	Same deal as the psychologist. However, a psychiatrist can prescribe medication. So, if you have to get a prescription filled, the person at the drug-store is going to know what medication you're taking. But, they won't know details.

Part two:
BODY

Chapter 7

Beauty

This is the hardest thing I'll have to tell you, and I'm not gonna beat around the bush. So here goes: the way you look *does* matter. And when you're a young woman, it matters a ton. Okay, so we didn't start the chapter off with the upbeat girl-power kind of statement you might have expected. But get over it, baby. We're going for the real deal, not a dream world.

The world can be shallow, confusing, and a source of stress when it comes to beauty. Younger and younger girls are driving themselves to be thin or getting plastic surgery because they're sure that if they *look* good, they'll *be* good. They'll feel pretty; other people will think they're pretty; and probably, good things will happen just because they look hot.

Here's the scoop: the shallow standard that convinces you beauty can make you a better person or change your life goes way back into history. Bring on the damsels in distress, the knights in shining armor, the tales of elegant queens and happily-ever-after endings in fancy castles with big, cool moats. We're off to the Middle Ages.

In the 1100–1300s, you were what you looked like. Beauty was the foolproof tool people used to figure out who was good, kind, and noble, and who was a downright wicked little punk.

Big Myth: Beauty is everything.

Real Deal: How you look isn't the biggest deal in the world, but it does matter.

Basically, what you sported on the outside was considered a reflection of your inner self. People imagined that inner attributes just sort of bubbled to the surface, broke loose, and covered the body from head to toe.

If you had goodness inside, then that's what bubbled up to the surface. On the other hand, people who were ugly ducklings were a different story. If their faces or bodies were nasty in any way, it was a sure sign of the evil that lay inside.

A whacked-out view of beauty? You bet. But we can learn from history and make something better of beauty today. We can make it work for us, being smart enough to know that beauty is only skin-deep. It won't make you rich and famous. It won't nab you the guy of your dreams or make you super-popular. And it definitely won't make you happy if there are other, bigger things troubling you deep inside.

Want the truth? Beauty's not a cure-all. There it is. Of course you don't have to be convinced of this just yet. Sometimes this lesson takes a while for us to learn. But do me a favor: lock this truth up somewhere tight in the back of your mind because you'll need it someday. All at once it will hit you, and you'll have to get your smarts on and admit that looks won't change your life.

This is (or will be) one of the best lessons you can learn. And if you learn it, you'll clear the way for beauty to become fun again. You'll create an environment where beauty is a tool you use to express yourself, not a prison in which you have to meet a standard that was set too high in the first place.

So in the rest of this chapter, we're going to move ahead and talk about beauty like we know the truth. We'll chat all about how beauty can be a powerful tool and *our* way to tell the world who we are.

What you won't find is a beauty checklist or a how-to guide. That's because there's never been just one path to beauty. There are as many ways to be beautiful and feel beautiful as there are girls on the globe. So instead of a bunch of dos and don'ts, we'll tackle hair, skin, and makeup in a way that lets you decide which ideas suit you best.

Outer Beauty Ins and Outs

The simple fact is this: getting beautiful—however we define beauty for ourselves—can give us a supercharged feeling of glam-power that will get us up and make us feel like a million bucks. Here's why . . .

Imagine you're hanging out in the quad during lunch, gabbing it up with your girls. You're all out on the tables. The guys you hang with are sitting over on the lawn. As you're talking, a girlfriend of yours launches into a story that's wicked-funny about some dude she saw on TV. Apparently the guy went so totally crazy for his team at a soccer match over in England that he bolted from the stands, ran onto the field, and headed straight toward the players' bench of the opposing team. All of a sudden the guy goes psycho, squirting them all in the face with his water bottle! So he cheers and squirts and cheers and squirts, then about fifty security guards and police all tackle the guy at once. He ends up in cuffs, but not before he lets out one last cheer, looks straight at the cops, aims what's left of his water bottle in their faces, and gives it a huge, heaving squeeze . . . like this!

Bam! Your girlfriend nails you straight in the face with a quick blast of water from her bottle, thinking it's beyond hilarious to catch you by surprise and squirt your face.

"Ha-ha," you say, slightly amused. "Very funny."

But just as you wipe off the water and give your girlfriend the joking evil eye, you look down at your hand and see nothing but a big, blue-black mess. Your friends are screaming with laughter—you're feeling confused. That is, until you catch a glimpse of yourself in a window, looking like a mutant creature from the black lagoon.

Mascara and eye shadow are streaked all across your face. The water has melted your outer beauty down, and you've just wiped what was left of it all over your face. Ugh.

Of course your friends think your new look makes the whole thing even funnier. They can't stop laughing for a second, and, frankly, their hysterics really aren't helping things at this point. They're pointing and laughing. You're embarrassed.

Oh, but don't even think that's the end of it. It gets so much worse. Just when you think you could die from being the center of attention because you look like such a freak, you notice all the boys over on the lawn have turned their heads to get a better look. Sure, you know the guys, and most of them are your friends, but it's really no consolation. You're standing there. Your face looks like the creature from the black lagoon. And all eyes are on you. Yikes!

Big Myth: My looks are who I am.

Real Deal: My looks influence the way I feel.

The moral of the story, ladies? It's obvious: the way you look on the outside influences the way you feel on the inside. One minute you're amped, having fun, and totally unconcerned with what you look like. The next minute you're self-conscious. You might become shy, frustrated, angry, or just plain embarrassed.

These kinds of emotions are what drive those fluttery feelings of insecurity you sometimes get. You're worried all eyes are on you, and this can make it tough to chill and just be yourself.

But if feelings of insecurity or nervousness can come from the way you look on the outside, so can feelings of confidence. Think about a day when you knew you looked great. When you hit your best look, you know it. You can feel it. You're comfortable, confident, and beautiful in your own skin. In short, you can just be yourself.

So let's take this knowledge and figure out how to use beauty to stay in this stride. Let's roll through the biggies—skin, hair, and makeup—to learn how to use outer beauty to show off the girl you are within and the girl you'd like to become as you grow up.

Skin

Teen angst over skin problems is so dramatic that sometimes even a bad soap opera can't compete. Too much goes into worries over pimples and other blemish spots because clear skin is in. Unfortunately, we don't all have a peaches-and-cream complexion. Because our bodies are all different, our skin is too. People who end up with great skin are just lucky. That's it. That's all. There's no magic to it. Good skin is just something in their genes.

For the rest of us, though, all is not lost. You can have clear skin too. You just have to take a few more steps to get it. Here's good advice for getting the best out of what God gave ya:

KEEPING YOUR FACE CLEAN = KEEPING YOUR HANDS OFF!

Clear complexions are a result of clear, unclogged pores. When you get zits, it's basically just a sign that you've got a clogged pore on your skin. So, anywhere you've got skin, you can get a zit. Sometimes there's dead skin cells clogging the pores, and sometimes there's oil called *sebum* (see-bum) clogging the pore. Either way, you're going to end up with a whitehead (when the clogged pore gets bacteria in it and closes up), a blackhead (when the clogged pore stays open and gets dirt on top of it), or a pimple (when the clogged pore closes up and bulges out from under the skin).

What to do when these blemishes arise? Simple: keep your hands off and your face clean. Acne scars look horrible— nobody likes 'em. And you can count on getting them if you're squeezing your zits. When you squeeze, you're breaking skin just as if you cut your knee or scraped your arm. You'll get a scab, it will take longer to heal, and you may end up with a dark patch or scar when it's all said and done.

For the day-to-day, get yourself into a regular routine of gentle facial cleansing. Wash gently, and don't use harsh scrubs or exfoliation. Another good way to keep your face clean is to use a cotton ball dipped in astringent to remove dirt from your face. You can buy expensive astringents if you want, but picking up a cheap bottle of a natural product called witch hazel from your local drugstore works just as well. Whether you wash, use astringent, or do both, always follow up with a facial moisturizer.

The last step to keeping skin clear is getting it flushed out. You've gotta get your water on, so drink up to keep yourself clean and clear. Dermatologists usually recommend drinking eight glasses of water a day. But what does that mean, exactly? What size glasses of water? The easy way to be sure you're getting your water's worth is to use this method: Think about sodas. You know the big ol' 44-ouncers you get? You'll need about one and a half of those full of water per day if you want to get what doctors recommend.

If after reading all this you still can't stand it and have to mess with your face, go the medication route. There are creams, washes, masks, and rubs that contain a medicine called "benzoyl peroxide" that can help reduce acne or the redness associated with it. Be sure to choose a medication that's right for your facial type. Dry skin will require one kind of medication, while girls with an oily complexion will require another. For extreme cases of acne, girls can get themselves to a skin doctor called a dermatologist who can prescribe something stronger.

In general, though, getting clear skin is just about being consistent, calm, and hanging in there. Bad skin rarely lasts forever.

SHE'S STINKY—AND IT'S NASTY

Just like they clog up your face, the oils put out by your body can also, well . . . clog up the air. Welcome to the world of body odor, or *B.O.*

When you hustle, hang out in the heat, or just get hot under the collar, your body unleashes a rush of oil and sweat. It's your body's way of cooling off, but it can make everybody a bit uneasy because of the ripe smell.

Here, two ideas can be helpful. First: let your nose be your guide and get yourself a deodorant that you like the smell of. You won't stop the sweat, but you will stop the odor and instead smell like the deodorant you select. Second: try to wear cotton clothing and underwear. Cute underpants might come in synthetic shiny and stretchy materials, but these don't absorb sweat and moisture well, and they can sometimes make you feel even sweatier because they don't let in enough air.

Hair

Who knew a zillion little tiny strands of hair could drive us so crazy when they're out of place, or make us feel so beautiful when we've got them styled just right? From tiny worries over choosing the ponytail over the straightener, to bigger worries over bad cuts and even worse color jobs, here's advice that'll help you out:

Motto: Go Wild but Don't Go Extreme

Whether you realize it or not, your hair can be the biggest source of beauty stress. A bad hair day often distracts you and keeps your mind occupied with something totally stupid but so incredibly frustrating that you can't get it out of your head.

So if one bad hair day can be a pain, imagine if that day seemed to last forever. Sure, you'd eventually get used to it, and the struggle to adjust might be good for you, but not that many people go out of their way to make stuff hard for themselves.

Chopping six inches off your hair might eventually feel liberating, but you'll freak when you first see it. Better to go inch by inch over a few months. Take your time when changing your hair. There's no hurry, and major mistakes are a pain.

Get your smarts on. Hair is fun to change, but take slow steps toward getting there.

Practice, Experiment, and Keep Up with Your Own Changes

My sister will kill me when she reads this, but it's vital information about hair that deserves to be let loose from the books of our family history and made available to every girl, far and wide. Here's the scoop:

Back in the day, my sister decided to wear her long, beautiful hair split right down the middle and woven into two braids. This in itself was just fine. She was workin' it, and the braids looked awesome.

That is, the braids looked awesome in fourth grade. But she wore them in fifth grade too. And in sixth grade. And in seventh. The weird thing was, the braids just didn't really seem to express who she had become by then. She had bloomed into an amazingly unique girl with a strong sense of herself and a bold view of the world. Her braids still matched her tender, compassionate heart. But in general, the braids just didn't go with her growing personality and interests.

So long story short here, ladies, keep an eye on the woman you're becoming. If outer beauty is your tool to express who you are within, don't be afraid to practice and experiment with new ideas.

Like we said earlier, though, don't go permanent and don't get all dramatic. But do practice with new looks or work on different styles as your tastes change. Growing up means changing tastes. Just because you liked having bangs in seventh grade doesn't mean you'll still think they're cool your sophomore year of high school. Changing your mind (and your hair) like this is par for the course.

Makeup

Makeup is where most girls go wrong . . . seriously wrong. Trying to look more mature, girls get in the habit of thinking lots of "product" (beauty-speak for makeup) will give them an older, more sophisticated look. This can work, sometimes. Like, for example, if you have Hilary Duff's professional makeup stylist working on you. But for the average girl, getting too much product on your face just ends up looking bad—it's either a bit trashy or a big-time eyesore. Get into the habit of believing some new things about makeup by reading the advice that follows. There are more uses for makeup than just trying to look older or going glam.

USE MAKEUP AS A FORM OF EXPRESSION, NOT A MASK

Listen up, now, ladies, because I'm about to drop the most important piece of information you'll ever learn when it comes to makeup: more isn't better. It's just more. It's not about how much makeup you put on—it's about what you use and the way you use it. Too much of any product makes girls look cakey and fake.

When it comes to makeup, your best bet—if your parents allow you to wear it—is to choose a few colors or styles that really show off what kind of person you are. For example, let's say you're the outspoken center of attention. If so, go for shine, sparkle, glitter, or other eye-catching products that match your personality. But what if you're more interested in a toned-down approach? What if you're just using makeup to give you that "healthy glow"? Try using a lightweight foundation and applying it with a soft, damp makeup sponge—you'll get great coverage that looks really natural. Throw on a light dose of neutral colors for your eyes and lips, and maybe a little bronzer on your cheeks to finish off the look.

Either route you choose, shoot for keeping your makeup as simple as possible. Aim to make your *face* an expression of who you are, not your makeup. Don't hide your face with a lot of products.

Keep Your Tool Set Clean

Because makeup applicators like sponges and brushes touch various parts of our face, they can spread bacteria from one place to another. One example is sharing mascara. You can actually pass eye infections from one person to another by sharing a mascara wand. This goes for other kinds of makeup products, too, like lipstick.

Other potential problems come from bacteria. Dirty makeup sponges or applicators can add dirt and oil to your face. Remember our talk about acne and zits? Bingo. Here's one place where you can keep an eye out and cut down the amount of unnecessary bacteria you bring in contact with your skin.

Change with the Seasons

One of the best parts about makeup is that it's cheap and comes in about a million-zillion colors and styles. This means every girl who likes to go the makeup route has tons of choices when it comes to changing her look.

Try going seasonal by matching your makeup to the time

of year. Get natural for summer with nudes and beiges. Get in the spirit for fall and the new school year with burgundies and browns, or just match your look to the seasons of your soul. Wear colors and looks that match the way you're feeling inside.

Deeper Than Our Skin

Here's the part of this chapter that probably sounds a lot like something your mom would say: it's not about how you look; it's about who you are. It's worth taking time to wrap this chapter with a mini-dose of this truth just to make sure we're on track with the good, the bad, and the ugly of beauty.

Big Myth: Makeup defines who I am.

Real Deal: Makeup expresses who I am.

For us, outer beauty is skin-deep. It's *our* tool, used *our* way, to say what we want about *our*selves. After all, outer beauty—no matter how great it all ends up looking in the end—is just a cheap, replaceable, shallow cover for what's really special, tucked inside. Even when we're feeling the worst ever about the way we look, deep down we know that looks are just skin-deep.

I know, I know . . . trying to believe that can be tough. In fact, it can be impossible, especially today. I live in the same world you do. I go to the same stores. I see the same advertisements. I watch the same television shows and movies. The beauty standard is set so ridiculously high that I sometimes feel defeated too.

But what I try to remember is that my look is mine. If I don't look like a supermodel, so what? All the trying in the world won't get me there. I like to eat, I'm not six feet tall, and I'm well into triple-digits on the scale now that I've matured into womanhood. That's just me—it's the way God designed me.

When I remind myself about this, I can feel beautiful on the outside by setting my own beauty standard. I go for the makeup and hair that make me feel like me, because nothing can beat how beautiful a girl feels when she's in her own skin.

But we gals have another secret weapon too. This is where our family or good friends come in. We need them to help us step back from the situation and get a handle on what's real: us. We're more than what we look like. Our clothes—even expensive ones—might seem really important, but they'll never measure up in importance to what's inside our minds, bodies, and souls. We're what's real, and our family and friends can remind us of that. They're the people who draw out the best in us. And when I say "the best," I'm not talking about our best look. Nope. What I'm talking about are our best inner qualities.

When you're down on yourself, hang out with a friend who makes you feel great on the inside and have a good laugh. Take a walk with your mom, and chat about a hobby you share or a memory that makes you both feel good. Pick up a ball or racket and go out with a friend who shares a love of sports with you. Or why not take yourself and a sibling somewhere that's just "yours." Find a secret spot where you two can team up, talk about problems, and remind one another about the strengths you have on the inside, like honesty, humor, or trustworthiness.

Beauty: Good, Better, Best

So here we are at the end of our chapter on beauty. Let's do two things: check out something we can use from the Bible to keep us centered on what beauty is for, and cut to the chase to bang out a list to see what we've learned at a glance. That way, when you're feeling like you need to check your head when it comes to beauty issues, you can flip straight here and get centered on what counts: you and God.

Big Myth: My looks draw out my best qualities.

Real Deal: Friends and family draw out my best qualities.

Okay, first let's get to the Bible. Beautiful people are everywhere, if you haven't noticed. Abraham's wife, Sarah, was a total bombshell. Bathsheba was an absolute beauty. And the Song of Solomon features a singer going on and on about the beautiful this and beautiful that of the woman he's in love with.

But the Bible also puts out a clear warning about the limits of beauty: beauty is passing. This little gem of wisdom is found in Proverbs 31 and should keep us grounded. Looks are fun to play with. But in the end, they'll be over someday. So if we organize our self-worth around what we look like on the outside, we're going to be out of luck. Better to build self-worth around something permanent, like our character, talents, or hobbies.

Okay, second. Let's get to what we've learned about beauty. Here goes:

- How you look *does* matter. But it's not *everything*.
- Outer beauty is a tool you use, not a prison in which you have to meet a standard that was set too high in the first place.
- Growing into a woman means accepting outer beauty biggies like pimples and stretch marks as a part of your growing body.

- Hair and makeup can reflect who we are inside. We can use them to express how we're changing, maturing, and growing as girls.
- Our looks are *an expression* of who we are, not *the definition* of who we are.
- Being beautiful on the outside feels great. But our real, true best self is brought out by our family and friends, not our looks.

Fashion

Fashion is a fun way to wrap up our personalities and present them to the world. Whether we sport a T-shirt or a tailored suit, our fashion choices are one way for us to show the wider world a bit about who we are.

Because we go to school, run errands, go out to dinner, hang with our friends, and do all sorts of stuff every day that puts us—and our fashion sense—right in the middle of the public eye, choices about what to wear can sometimes seem overwhelming. What to wear can even seem like the biggest deal in the world. Have you ever had one of those days where you try on six different outfits before you leave the house? We worry that if we don't make the right fashion choices, we might be rejected, unpopular, or just plain unhappy with ourselves.

This whole situation is a bit like wrapping up gifts or presents for friends. Usually when we wrap a gift, we take the time to make sure it looks great. After all, what kind of gifts do people get excited about the most? Not the ones that are all torn-up and nasty. No way. People go crazy for the gifts that shine, look beautiful, and seem special in some way.

Compare this to how we think about fashion and what we wear. We take time to make sure our look is great. We love it when people notice, and dressing in particular ways can make us look, feel, or seem amazingly beautiful or fancy.

We use outer beauty, like clothes and fashion, as a kind of wrapping for our bodies. We focus on outer beauty to make ourselves look (and feel) special and beautiful. Sometimes we do this for ourselves. Sometimes we do this for others, like at an event for our parents.

Unfortunately for some girls, they put too much stock in the way they look. They confuse what's being worn on the outside with what was created by God on the inside, in their hearts, minds, and souls.

When this happens, a girl might spend a ton of time worrying about how she looks only to discover that nothing has really changed in her life. Everything is pretty much the same (except she's got some nice, nice clothes), and all the killer things she hoped would come to her because she looked so great never really materialized in her life. No extra popularity. No spot on the honor roll. No date to the prom. That's the reality of superficial things like fashion. It's just wrapping. It can't change our lives.

But just because fashion can't change your life all by itself doesn't mean it's good for nothing. No way! Here are three great things fashion can do for you:

1. It can get you psyched for the part you'd like to play in life.
2. It can give you a way to express a million different shades of your personality.
3. It can be replaced in a jiffy. Tired of a look or want a change? No sweat, because fashion can be replaced.

Getting Psyched for Your Part in Life

Discovering what kind of fashion works for you is one way to get yourself ready for the part you'd like to play in life. Why? Because the way you look outside can determine how you feel about yourself inside.

But listen close here. I'm not saying that the way we look is *what we are* on the inside. I'm saying that what we wear can sometimes determine *how we feel* about ourselves inside.

Your best bet is to use your instincts about what feels right when you're getting dressed. Listen to your inner voice. If you don't feel comfortable in an outfit when you're by yourself looking in the mirror, you definitely aren't going to feel comfortable in that outfit in front of lots of people.

By listening to yourself, you can decide on a comfortable style that's right for you. Then you can pair that style up with different stuff you do, or events you'll be attending. This is the best way to feel confident. You'll have a look that works for you but is also right for the events in your life. Why not give the following suggestions a try?

THE EVENT: STUDENT ELECTION SPEECH

The Point. Use fashion to communicate a sense of smarts.

The Feel. Confident and intelligent. It's a day to have your mind in high gear and your voice heard. Go for style, but make what you have to say the center of attention by playing your clothes and makeup down a notch.

Big Myth: What's outside is real.

Real Deal: What's outside is wrapping.

The Look. Professional and pulled together.

The Clothes. Go for a great skirt or pair of pants, but say no to really tight styles or casual stuff, like denim. Collared shirts or tops that look a little bit preppy help to make outfits look clean, confident, and professional. Solid colors are the easiest to match for both the top and bottom here. And if you stick with solid colors, you nix the chance of people being blinded, paralyzed, and unable to hear your speech because you've abused everyone's tender little eyeballs with an outrageous print, pattern, or design on your clothes.

The Accessories. Go for accessories that scream . . . well, nothing. You want toned-down accessories that are fairly standard (like small earrings or a small necklace) and don't distract attention away from you or what you have to say. One thing you might consider (if you've got 'em) is putting on your specs. Glasses give that grown-up, smarty, Tina Fey kind of feel to an outfit.

The Hair & Makeup. You can do your hair back, or leave it down. Just be sure it's tidy and not too wild. For makeup, stick with neutral tones on the eyes, lips, and cheeks to make sure your cosmetics aren't competing with your speech.

THE EVENT: WEEKEND PARTY

The Point. Use fashion to communicate a sense of your inner creativity and spirit.

The Feel. Fun, funky, and confident.

The Look. Fun, free, and relaxed.

The Clothes. Go for shorts or a pair of capri cargos. Skirts seem like a great party choice, but some skirts (especially really short ones) limit your ability to have fun because you're so worried about flashing your underwear to people by accident. For a matching top, if it's warm you might think about wearing a tank. They're fun and come in all kinds of shapes, cuts, and styles.

The Accessories. Party accessories are great because they can get funky and give your look an extra bang for its buck. One easy way to achieve this bang is to go for a necklace. Find one that features some sort of singular charm that dangles from the front to attract attention. Charms that have been made with interesting patterns or are made in interesting shapes are almost always a winner.

The Hair & Makeup. You can do your hair up, leave it down, or try adding some cute little braids for that retro look. Parties are a place where any hair goes. For makeup, go for something different. Why not try something like slightly smoky eyes for a night party, or glitter-infused lip gloss for super shine during a day party.

THE EVENT: SPORTS GAME OR MATCH

The Point. Use fashion to communicate a sense of athleticism and independence.

The Feel. Fit, prepared, and ready to take on the competition.

The Look. Strong and athletic.

The Clothes. Here you'll probably be wearing your team's uniform, so picking clothes isn't a big deal. But make sure all the parts of your uniform are clean—from the socks on up.

The Accessories. Um, are you kidding? You're going to play sports, right? Leave the bracelets, earrings, and other accessories at home. It's a safety issue and a sports issue. Keep yourself accessory-free to play your best game and keep everyone on the field a bit safer.

The Hair & Makeup. Go for a ponytail, braid, or other updo for your hair so you can keep your hair out of your face and concentrate on playing your best. Make your play the star of the game, not your hair. For makeup, choose waterproof products, like mascara, for your eyes and go for a lip gloss that packs a sun-protective punch (SPF 15). Also, don't forget the sunscreen. Tans are great, but when you're older, you'll find that skin cancer's not. Seriously.

THE EVENT: BIG-TIME DANCE OR PROM

The Point. Use fashion to make you look (and feel) like a modern-day Cinderella.

The Feel. Special, beautiful, and like the belle of the ball.

The Look. Absolutely beautiful.

The Clothes. Go for a dress, for sure. Big-time dances and proms are some of the best places to live out those cheesy-but-fun fantasies where you get to be the belle of the ball. Don't shy away from silky, rich, sumptuous fabrics. Instead, indulge yourself in something that makes you feel magical. Just make sure you buy a size and style that's big enough so you can get your dance on. The prom is a real downer when you can't even hit the floor because your dress is too tight to move a muscle.

The Accessories. Go for clean, delicate, and simple with a bit of glam. Just know that jewelry is like makeup: more isn't better, it's just more. Instead of getting all iced out, see if your mom, aunt, or grandma has something unique you could borrow. Just keep things simple—nobody needs to rock platinum from head to toe.

The Hair & Makeup. Most girls go for the updo when it comes to hair for big events like these. But just like the dress you choose, the whole point is beauty, magic, and the freedom to go for a look that expresses a part of who you are. Why not try braiding beads into your hair, using ribbons or ties that match your dress, or changing your style. If you always wear your hair straight, go for some curls. If you're always sporting curls, smooth it out and go for a straight 'do.

For makeup, it's the same deal. There's no need to go heavy here. Go for creative ideas all geared toward a classic, beautiful look that's clean, fresh, and shows off your best features. Your dress, accessories, and hair will be all styled-out and on parade as well, so you don't need to worry about getting too dramatic with the makeup. Think of it as a companion piece to an overall look, not as the key element that will make the look all on its own.

A Million Shades of Personality

Getting good at wrapping yourself with choices that work for you is relatively easy. You can use your creativity to create different exteriors with just a little practice and a bit of trial and error.

This is great news because it allows you to let your real self shine through. Every look you see another girl sporting—from super-square librarian to the wildest punk—is offering you a little reflection of what's inside of her. So when we experiment with outer beauty, we're experimenting on a project that's going to let us express a part of ourselves to the world.

But if the world is going to get a dose of who you are through what you choose to wear, it's worth your while to break out your brainpower on this issue. The person you are and the person that other people think you might be is often based on the way you look. It's a big factor in how people first think about you. Being sure that you project an image of who you are inside by what you wear outside is something you should pay attention to.

For example, think about any celebrity. Then ask yourself what kind of outer wrapping she usually uses. Does she usually wrap herself in stuff you consider cool, slutty, trendy, sexy, or uptight?

Next, ask yourself what kind of person you imagine this celebrity is in real life. You know, ask yourself what you think that person would be like if you met her. Do you imagine she'd be nice to you? Do you imagine she'd be really smart? Or do you imagine she'd be kind of shallow, sexually loose, or even look down on you?

Of course these thoughts are all just imaginary. We can't tell what kind of person someone is just by the way she looks. But when I asked you to imagine what these people would be like in real life, was that hard for you? Probably not.

The reason it wasn't hard is because you see celebrities on the plasma screen and in the movies, day in and day out. You've seen them so often that you've come up with opinions on who they are. This is an opinion based on looks. It's based on how celebrities have wrapped their package and presented it to you and the rest of the world.

This might not be fair, but it's life. It's unrealistic to think that when you show up to school in a super-short, low-rise miniskirt and a tiny crop top with no bra, people are going to rush over in droves, asking you to tutor them in their advanced-placement algebra assignments. Instead, most people who see you will probably think . . . well, they'll probably think lots of things. But you can pretty much bet these things won't be about how smart, nice, or fun you are.

Take this reality seriously. It happens at school when we're young, but it will continue to happen as we get older too. Whether we go to college or land a job as a working adult, we can count on the fact that what we wear can sometimes speak louder than what we say or who we are on the inside.

Match your mind to your wardrobe and you can't go wrong. One way to do this is to use fashion to express what's inside you. Here are a few tips on how to make what's inside fashionable on the outside too:

Use Clothes as Your Costume

Let's face it: being trendy won't ever go out of style. But the good news is that girls have gone through so many trends in the last few decades that today you can sport nearly any style you want and no one is going to get all bent over it.

Because of this diversity, the clothes aren't nearly half as important as how and when you wear them. So treat your clothes like a costume. Mix your look up or match it to your mood. Anything goes because personal style goes way farther than seasonal trends.

For example, if you're a preppy kind of girl, then stay true to it. Go for solids, like capri khakis or other flat-front, slim-legged pants, and pair them with an adorable short-sleeved button-up shirt with a funky collar. There's a ton of preppy choices that can look stylish.

On the other hand, maybe you're more of a free-spirited girl or you like to get retro with your look. If so, then take a U-turn from the preppy choices and go for pure funk or fifties. You can mix-and-match clothing from vintage shops, independent stores, and the shops you like at the mall to come up with something that works for you.

If your look is yet to be defined or you get a headache even thinking about fashion, then your best bet is to take a look around. Use other people's style as a guide. Note the colors, fabrics, and cuts that appeal to you.

What's Really Important: Mind, Heart, Soul

The best outfits in the world are still just a cheap wrapper. Learning this lesson now will help as you grow toward woman-hood and try to navigate the world of fashion. The reason why we want to work so hard to distinguish between what's out-side and what's inside is simple: What's outside is wrapping. What's inside is real.

That's right. The real deal—you—doesn't come in a new color every spring. The real you isn't a trendy exterior—no way, no how. The real you is what's tucked on the inside, and it's irreplaceable.

It does a girl good to remind herself of this fact. Sometimes (with all the noise, pictures, and pressures of the world today) we begin to think that we're the sum of our parts. We can be tricked into thinking that the amount of stuff we have adds up to how good we are as people, or how special we should consider ourselves.

But the truth is that all stuff you can collect or wear, including fashion, is replaceable. It's something temporary, something that can be thrown away in two seconds flat. What's inside you, however, is here to stay. So, repeat the mantra with me: what's outside is wrapping; what's inside is real.

Say it again and again if you have to, but be sure to use this phrase to help put fashion in its proper place—on the outside, as a form of creativity, and as an expression of the girl who lies within.

Chapter 9

New Developments

Okay . . . try to stay calm.

You're in class. You're wearing a skirt. And all of a sudden you're getting that feeling in your underwear. You're almost positive that you've started your period and that you're about two seconds away from having it leak onto your clothes.

Options here?

1. Cross your legs and squeeze for your life! Maybe pressure will stop it, or at least slow it down.
2. Find so many long-winded questions to ask after class (from your seat, of course) that every single person in the room is so ridiculously bored from listening to you they finally have to leave—including your teacher. Then hit it to the rest room—ASAP—with no one around to see the leak.
3. PANIC!

Just about every girl has either been in this situation or will be. It's your period. And if you didn't know it was about to drop, you can really be caught off guard. You can be freaked out. You can be thrown into a panic. You can be super embarrassed and simply want to die, right there on the spot.

Getting your period is just one of the many new developments that signal your move away from being a little girl. On your way to womanhood you'll also pick up breasts, pubic hair, and some additional weight and fat. You'll be getting feelings or sensations all over your body that you've never had before.

If no one has hit you with this information, it might be a bit much to handle. It's a bumpy ride into womanhood, and it's a long one too. Most girls need about five years to work out all the kinks and reach a stage where their bodies are done developing the things they'll need for womanhood.

The two sections in this chapter will get you the info on all the stuff that will happen during this time. We're jumping in to get answers to the biggest physical changes that you'll be experiencing: the growth of breasts and the start of your period.

New Stuff

There's a ton of new stuff that's happening inside and outside of your body right now. Let's just jump right in and do it by sections. We'll just hit you with a bunch of answers to the biggest questions most girls have.

BREASTS

Q: **My girlfriends are just as obsessed with boobs right now as the guys seem to be. Is there some kind of connection? Why all the boob-obsession?**

A: In America you can't take more than sixty steps without seeing some kind of picture or ad with a woman's breasts as the focal point. So when girls start to develop breasts, it can be hard not to get into the habit of watching their growth. It's kind of like a comparison thing. When new stuff pops up on our bodies (literally, in this case), we're going to be lost in our own little world of wonder for a while.

Guys get lost in this world, too, but for different reasons.

As you both are maturing toward adulthood, you're both also maturing toward fully developed sex drives. Boys are simply attracted to your chest because it's a natural part of their sex drive. With girls' chests developing all around them, it's almost more than they can take sometimes.

Q: Argh! My breasts are two different sizes. When's the other one going to catch up?

A: First things first: only you are noticing the asymmetry of your breasts. It's not like you're walking down the hall and people are like, "No way. Look how huge her right boob is compared to her left one . . . it's like a giant monster! Run for it, before it attacks us!"

The second thing you should know is that breasts are just one thing your body is working on developing right now. For a time your body might work on one breast, then move on to something else, then come back to work on the other breast. So the second rule of thumb is to be patient and see if things even out.

Big Myth: If I make my boobs look bigger, I'll get more guys.

Real Deal: If you make your boobs look bigger, you'll attract immature guys who may only want you for your body.

The last thing you should know is that time won't change everything. You may wait and wait, only to find that your boobs are destined to be uneven. In some cases, your breasts may vary by a cup size or more. If this describes your situation— or if you just can't stand to have unequal breasts—check out these options that might help:

Padded Bras. Speak up and let your mom, grandma, aunt, or whoever takes you to buy undergarments, know that you feel insecure about the way your breasts look. Then use their help to find a padded bra with enough of a shape to make it look like your breasts are even. You try the bras on; they'll tell you when everything looks equal.

Inserts. Recently girls have been able to buy inserts that tuck into the bottom edge of a bra. These inserts can be large, medium, or small. And they're usually washable, too, so you can throw them in with your regular laundry. Plastic varieties of inserts are also on the market now, and they work the same way. Just choose a size and tuck it into your bra, on the bottom side, beneath your breast.

Q: **My nipples and the circle around them are getting really dark. Is this normal?**

A: The area around your nipple is called the *areola* (say it with me: air-e-o-la). When it changes in shape or color, it's a sign that your breasts are maturing. Underneath your breast, on the inside, your body is creating lots of milk ducts, fat deposits, and other things you'll need if you're a mom someday and you need to nurse a baby. So if you're seeing your nipples become longer and pointed, and you're also seeing your areola becoming darker, this is just the way the outside of your body shows what's going on inside.

Q: **It seems like I'm always spilling out the top or sides of my bras, and you can see it bulging out through my clothes. Am I wearing the wrong size or something?**

A: Could be the wrong size. Or it could be that your breasts would fit better in a different cut of bra. When you get to the lingerie department, have a saleslady help you fit yourself to the right bra for you. Here are some options for you in terms of bra style:

Soft Cup. Seamless, smooth, and lightweight. Soft-cup bras make your breasts look as natural as possible and usually have elastic rather than wire running underneath your breasts. If you find that you're spilling out of a bra, it may be because the elastic of a soft-cup bra isn't enough support.

Underwire. This kind of bra might seem uncomfortable, but it's sturdy and holds most girls in pretty snug. The underwire is enclosed in soft material and fits just below the breast to assure that everything is supported and stays in place.

Push-Up. If you're spilling out of a bra, it may be because your breasts are too large for a push-up bra. Push-ups give girls with smaller breasts an extra bit of lift and shape. But if you're a gal with larger breasts, you may be getting too much boost from this kind of bra. You might find your breasts spilling up and over (and maybe out and down too!).

Sports. Some girls consider life a sport. So why not wear a bra to match? Sports bras come in lots of sizes and shapes, but most look like skintight tank tops. There's no spilling out, and sports bras come with ample elastic support for each breast. The only downside is that sports bras sometimes flatten breasts out.

Minimizer. These are bras that are designed to do nothing but make your breasts look smaller. If you're a girl who is self-conscious about her big chest or you just don't seem to fit in other styles, you may find a minimizer a comfortable option. But be sure you get one that you can be active in. Minimizer bras can be thick and come with substantial straps.

Q: **My friend is only thirteen, and she already has huge breasts. I'm a year older and still haven't really developed yet.**

A: Puberty starts and ends at different ages for different girls. The difference between you and your friend just has to do with how fast the puberty-clock is ticking inside each of your bodies. It may have to do with race too. Recent studies show that girls of one race, like African-Americans, will get a dose of the grown-up weight, fat, and curves that create full breasts, hips, and thighs sooner than girls of other races, like Caucasians or Asians. This all has to do with how soon something called *estrogen* (ess-tro-gen) shows up in a girl's body. Estrogen is a hormone your body will produce as soon as your reproductive organs (your ovaries) go into full swing. Breasts are designed by God to come in every shape and size. There's none better and none worse. It's not that I expect you to buy this right off the bat, but you do need to hear it as often as possible. Just because girls get obsessed with making their boobs bigger, firmer, or more attractive doesn't mean a darn thing for you. Your breasts are fine the way they are.

Q: My breasts really hurt right now. Why am I so tender?

A: When you're about to start—or are on—your period, the hormones in your body go through a change. This means you've got hormones going every which way through your bloodstream, making some parts of your body extra sensitive. Your breasts can be one of these parts. But you don't need to get worried about it—it's only a temporary sensation. After your period you'll probably find that your breasts go back to feeling like normal.

You can try a few things to help sensitive breasts. One option is to wear clothes that aren't fitted, tight, or restrictive during your period. Also, you can choose soft fabrics, like cotton, to minimize the amount of rubbing and friction that stretchy fabrics, like Lycra, can cause. And last, it may feel better to skip wearing your bra during this week (if that's a modest choice). The underwire, straps, and other parts of your bra can be annoying if you've got tender breasts. So try switching to something less confining, like a camisole, sports bra, or undershirt instead.

PERIODS

Q: Nobody really went over the details with me. Why do girls get periods, and what are they?

A: Inside your body you've got two *ovaries* (over-ies). Each ovary is an egg-making machine. And each month—after you've reached puberty—one ovary or the other will get an egg ready.

Ready for what? Ready to be fertilized. When you mature and reach puberty, your body becomes capable of reproduction—you can have babies. So, because the egg is the half a woman contributes toward making a child, the ovaries send along an egg each month as a sign that the body is working properly and ready to reproduce.

After the ovary has got the egg all prepped, it sends it into the *fallopian* (fa-lope-ee-un) tube. This is called "ovulation." From the fallopian tube, the egg travels toward your uterus. This trip usually takes about four days, and some girls see bits of spotting or blood during this time. Other girls see nothing and have little to no pain.

While the egg is making its way into your uterus, the ovary is still going strong to prep everything. The egg is done being made, but it needs somewhere to land. So the ovary signals the uterus to build up a lining that will cushion the egg once it arrives there. With the spongy lining in place, the egg can coast down into the uterus and chill.

Big Myth: I just have to grin and bear it if my period leaks through my pants.

Real Deal: I just have to keep a long-sleeved shirt or sweater in my locker to tie around my waist in case of emergencies.

This is where the baby or no-baby part happens. When women become pregnant, it's because a man's sperm meets up with the egg at this point. Or it could be that a man's sperm met up with the egg on its way down the fallopian tube. Or, it could be that a man's sperm was hanging around (male sperm can live four to six days inside a woman) and met up with the egg on its way by.

Either way, what's gone on is that a sperm met the egg, worked its way inside the egg, and has fertilized the egg. Nine months later—with God's blessing and direction—a baby is born.

When a woman has her period, it's because a sperm never met up with the egg. The egg traveled down the fallopian tube and hung out in the uterus, but no sperm came to fertilize it. So the egg and the spongy lining both disintegrate. Then they're flushed out by your body and you get your period.

Your period can last anywhere from two to eight days. And, most girls can count on it coming again in about twenty-six to thirty-seven days. Other girls will have "irregular" periods, meaning they'll bleed at different times and for different lengths. But for most girls, periods will happen for about the same number of days, during the same week each month.

Try getting into the habit of marking your period on your calendar to see what's up with your cycle. A little red dot, or a circle, on the first day that you bleed can be day one. Then use a little black X when you don't see any more blood. That will mark the final day of your cycle. Over time you'll probably notice a pattern. Then you can be prepared and plan ahead of time for the days you'll have your period.

Q: I can't stop feeling emotional and getting worked up over stuff when I'm on my period. Sometimes I get cramps too. Is it just me?

A: Nope, it's not just you. Many girls report feeling cranky when they're just about to have their period and while it's going on too. Doctors usually attribute this to something called "premenstrual syndrome," or PMS.

All sorts of stuff counts as PMS, according to doctors. Here's just a few: bloating or feeling like you're fat or puffy, headaches, stomachaches, nausea, feeling breast tenderness, being irritable or stressed-out, wanting to eat a lot, or breaking out.

So some of this stuff is physical, and some of it is mental. Just know that having a period is a big deal for some girls. Don't stress if you need to deal with stuff slower, be in a more quiet environment, or just take a break more often when you're having your period.

Q: Tampons are scary to me, but pads feel lumpy. Why can't I get comfortable?

A: This might be a bummer, but here goes anyway: having your period isn't about being comfortable. Periods are a pain. But periods are also a girls-only kind of deal and something that you'll eventually get used to and maybe even feel privileged to have.

Even though girls have two different choices about how to safely catch the blood flow that results from having a period, neither is a dream fit. Both options have good and bad qualities. Let's run them down and go over how each option can be used:

A Girl's Two Choices	Pads	Tampons
What's up with it.	Most girls start with pads because they're easy. You just peel and stick 'em right on your underpants to catch the blood from your period as it leaves your body.	Tampons can be a bit scary at first. You have to ease them gently inside your vagina, where they'll absorb the blood and tissue from your period. They can be difficult for some girls to insert at first.

What kind to get.	If you don't know how heavily your body usually bleeds during your period, try buying a sampler pack of pads. In the pack, you'll find a few thin (light flow) pads, medium (regular flow) pads, and heavy-duty (heavy flow) pads. Then, once you figure out which one works for you, it's as simple as getting them at the store each month.	Tampons come with and without applicators. Applicators help you slide the tampon into place. The box will show you how. You just push up gently on one end of the applicator, and the tampon is inserted. Non-applicator tampons have a place to put your finger for insertion. Tampon size varies, just like pad size. Smaller tampons are for light days of bleeding. Larger tampons are for heavier days.
What's good about it.	The good part about pads is that they're simple. Just peel and stick the pad to your underpants. You can buy pads that have flaps (usually called "wings") on each side to cut down on blood that might accidentally leak on your panties. And pads come in different scents too. If you like to mask the smell of your period, perfumed pads can help out.	Because tampons are inside your body, you can swim, wear fitted clothing, and be more active without worrying about a bulky pad getting in your way.
What stinks about it.	Two main problems—leakage and comfort. First, pads can be messy. You could end up getting spots or stains on your underpants—or worse-case scenario, leak right onto your clothes. Second, they're heavy, lumpy, and can give you rashes. For some girls they're just really uncomfortable because they can come loose or get twisted or bunched. And many girls just don't like the fact that they don't seem as clean as tampons.	Tampons can be awkward. The first time you use one might hurt a little. A second bummer is the risk of getting "Toxic Shock Syndrome," or TSS. Hardly any girls ever get TSS, but it can be really dangerous. Girls get TSS from bacteria that build up inside their bodies as a result of leaving a tampon in too long.

Q: My friend told me that I shouldn't use a tampon because I'd lose my virginity. Why would she say that—is it true?

A: Your girlfriend's just being dramatic here. Yes, a tampon does go inside of your vagina—the same place a man's penis goes when people have sex. But a tampon is not a penis. You aren't having sex when you use a tampon. You're catching the blood and tissue that your body naturally sheds each month as you mature into a woman.

Don't sweat it—you're definitely still a virgin if you use a tampon.

Big Myth: If I use a tampon, I won't be a virgin anymore.

Real Deal: If I use a tampon, I will still be a virgin.

Q: At my school I heard a girl talking about having to go to the doctor after she got her period. What's that all about?

A: When a girl gets her period, it means her reproductive system is up and running now. Like any system in your body, this system needs regular checkups to stay healthy and make sure everything's all right. The doctor who performs these checkups is called the "ob-gyn," or gynecologist. This is a doctor who has been specially trained in gynecology (study of reproductive organs) and/or in obstetrics (pregnancy and childbirth).

Once you begin menstruating, it's a good idea to get into the habit of having a pap smear and some of the other tests that a gynecologist will perform. This will keep you clear of infections, diseases, or other irregularities that might come up.

Big Myth: Girls should have their period by the time they're sixteen.

Real Deal: Girls develop at different rates. Ask an adult if you're still showing no signs of puberty by age sixteen.

HAIR

Q: Is it just me, or do all girls have this much hair on their bodies? I feel like a crazy gorilla-girl.

A: Body hair, because it's new and can often be dark, thick, or curly, is a pretty big shock when we get it. What's worse is that sometimes this hair just doesn't seem to want to grow in the places we'd like it to most. The real deal is that hair is something all girls get. But not all girls get the same amount, color, thickness, or type of hair.

Some of this variation is related to your ethnicity. For example, girls of Asian descent usually end up with the lightest, thinnest, and least amount of hair.

But what to do with hair? Shave it? Pluck it? Wax it? Cut it? Leave it alone? In the end, it's all up to you. Just be sure to be safe if you choose to go about hair removal. Here's a quick guide to the most popular options:

SHAVING

It's: quick, cheap, and all you have to learn how to do is use a razor. Be sure to ask a parent before you shave (in case your family has rules about when shaving should begin), and try to choose a razor that's got plenty of girl-stuff in mind: flexible blades to bend over places like your knees, and lubrication strips to keep your skin from breaking out or drying up.

It Lasts For: shaving isn't permanent. You'll have to bust out the razor again each time the hair grows long again.

Lotion

It's: a leave-on process where you apply the lotion to the places on your body you'd like to remove hair from. Wait a few minutes, then rinse.

It Lasts For: about a week or so. Lotion works by getting rid of hair at the root, so it will grow back just like shaving. But because lotion gets rid of the hair a little bit farther down the root than shaving does, you'll get a few more days of smooth skin.

Waxing

It's: hot wax applied to your skin, then ripped off. With the wax applied, you let it attach to the root of the hair, then yank the hairs out by the root. Sound painful? It is. Waxing won't be so bad you can't bear it, but it's not smooth sailing. Get ready to be uncomfortable.

It Lasts For: one to three months. To be sure you're keeping your body safe and clean, it's best to have waxing done by a professional. Home waxing kits are messy, and they can also spread bacteria from place to place on your legs. This means you may end up with legs that are broken out in rashes, acne, or ingrown hairs.

Chapter 10

Sex and Sexuality

This is a chapter that a lot of you girls might like. First, it's a chapter about sex that's frank, up-front, and will tell it like it is. Second, it's got a ton of information you can read in private. Why's that a great thing? Because, let's face it, some of us don't live in homes where talk about sex is open and out on the table. We've got lots of questions, but not a whole lot of ways to communicate them to people around us.

For girls, talking about sex and sexuality can be tough. It can be even tougher for Christian girls. We're committed to keeping our bodies pure, but does that mean we're not supposed to ask any questions along the way? Does it mean that if we ask questions about sex, our parents will suspect that we're being tempted or have gone too far? Sometimes it can seem like that.

Knowing that you have a ton of questions but feeling like there's no good place to ask them can be frustrating. You may have thought about asking your parents before but then got too afraid, embarrassed, or worried about it to follow through. Or you may have thought about asking someone at your church and then changed your mind. After all, it's not like you're going to show up on Sunday and launch into sex talk with your youth pastor.

Okay, maybe it's just me, but there's about a 100 percent chance that I'd rather die than tell Pastor Chris about some guy I'm crushing on that I'm totally tempted to make out with. No way! I'd be way too embarrassed. Plus, I'd worry that he'd think I was . . . well, trashy. That, because I was tempted, I wasn't living up to the example a Christian girl should set regarding sex.

This is exactly why it can be so hard to get any questions answered about sex and sexuality. You may have some great adults in your life, but there's just some stuff you'd be too embarrassed to tell them—stuff you'd feel weird about if they knew.

If you feel this way, you're not alone, at all. Very few girls have adults in their lives that are cool enough to chat about sex with them. Though moms, dads, and other adults try, they just don't always make it into this "cool" zone. They're either too embarrassed themselves and never come to talk to you about sex, or when you go to talk to them about sex, it's really uncomfortable for both of you.

This is where a chapter like this comes in. First, we'll go through sexuality as a part of your body and a part of your development as a woman. Then we'll get to sex. To make this information easy to get, I've arranged the talk about sex in a question-and-answer format so you can skip right to the advice you need.

Sexuality

Q: Okay, if sex is something people do, then what's sexuality?

A: Well, it's a couple of things. First, *sexuality* refers to the fact that we're sexual beings. *Sexuality* is being interested in sex and the touching, kissing, and physical turn-ons that go with it. And second, *sexuality* is how into physical attraction you are. It's how much you like flirting, being flirted with, dressing in certain ways, checking out guys' bodies, and stuff like that.

What you should know about sexuality is that it's completely normal. Sexuality is one part of our mind-body-soul package. It's God-designed, and we're intended to use it. How we use it, though, is another question. And it's a question that will be answered—in part—by the way we confront what's happening in our bodies, the cultural stereotypes we buy into, and the friends we keep.

CONFRONTING YOUR BODY

What you do about your sexuality has a lot to do with the way you confront what's going on with your body. The fact is, you're growing into womanhood, and that means becoming a sexual being. Eventually, you'll most likely have a sexual relationship with your spouse and be able to bear children. So right now, the changes going on in your body are preparing you for this.

But remember that each girl is on her own timetable. Each girl's body develops differently, and girls are ready for different things at different times in their lives. For example, one of my friends ended up breaking up with her boyfriend because he and a bunch of other couples were going to have a kiss day. All the couples were going to kiss on campus at school every time they saw each other, like a kind of dare or a game. My friend wasn't having it. She just wasn't ready for the PDAs (Public Displays of Affection). In fact, she had just started dating. So she just wasn't ready to act that way. And you know what? Dumping her guy was a great choice for her at that stage. If you're not ready to date, get physical, or get into boys on the same level that your friends are, don't even sweat it. What each girl does with her own body is different. Getting physical, being into guys, and trying to navigate the ways our bodies and emotions are feeling is a huge job. Tackle it when you're ready. Deal with the role sexuality will play in your life when you're ready to face these issues and really give them some thought.

CULTURAL STEREOTYPES

The world of sex has a lot more to it than "doing it" or "not doing it." Of course you'd never know this by taking a look at the culture around you. Most TV shows feature characters that have sex. Most movies have a sex scene. Many songs sing about sex or wanting to have sex. But what about the rest of the stuff? What about dating and marriage? What about what happens after sex? What about the questions these people have before sex?

The before, after, and confusing parts are usually left out of our cultural stereotypes about sex. Mostly, all we see are characters who meet, say hi, crack a few jokes to each other, and then jump in the sack and do it.

What's missing is sexuality. The bit of flirting we see between characters can't show us the full range of sexual feelings that people really experience when they become aware of the role sexuality plays in their lives. So, if you buy into cultural stereotypes, you're buying into a very limited picture of what sexuality can mean in your life.

The real deal is that most girls begin to feel a spark, shock, or tingle somewhere deep in the pit of their stomachs or in their vaginas when their sexuality kicks in. These kinds of feelings are usually called "being turned on." Feelings like these are a sign that your brain is sending messages to your body to get you ready for sex.

It might send messages about things you find attractive, or it may send messages of curiosity. But in general, when your sexuality kicks in, you're on the way to womanhood. You'll be curious, interested, and maybe even fascinated with stuff that has to do with sex.

THERE ARE DIFFERENT RESPONSES TO BEING TURNED ON

Sometimes girls like the feeling. They become really interested in it. These girls might experiment with trying to make other people feel the same way too. They might be really into flirting or being close to boys. Or they might dress or act in ways that will attract guys around them. This experimentation is one way for a girl to explore a part of herself that's becoming a woman. But there's also a downside to getting too focused on wanting guys to show they're interested in you, or aiming to draw a lot of sexual attention. Someday down the line, you're gonna end up in the arms of a guy you really like. You may even marry him, eventually. But, if you've set up a pattern where a part of you totally feeds off the attention you get when you dress sexy or flirt it up with other guys, your relationship could suffer. He may get jealous. You may end up being the center of trash-talking gossip because of the way you act. The spark of sexuality that's fun to play with when girls are able to draw attention isn't meant to turn into a blazing fire for every guy to see. Eventually, you'll want to offer only one guy this spark.

Not all girls want to jump right in. Some girls feel shy or private about these new emotions and physical sensations. If this describes you, don't worry about it. Sexuality is really powerful, and it's best to let two things guide you through this time in your life: your inner voice and your commitment to Christ. Your inner voice will tell you how comfortable you are acting or dressing in certain ways. You might feel weird wearing "sexy" clothes or trying to get guys to notice you. If so, listen to this voice inside yourself. There's no need to hurry up. And when it comes to your commitment to Christ, hurrying isn't going to help the situation, anyway. If you've given your promise to God to keep your body pure, then hurrying to explore sexuality and the feelings it revs up inside will only make this commitment harder. You'll be put in way more situations where you have to speak up, draw boundaries, say no when guys ask for things, like your virginity, that you've already agreed to keep for your future and yourself.

Being this firm, this clear, and this committed to your promise to your body and to Christ can be really tough for some girls. So whenever you choose to examine your sexual feelings, just know that it will take a bit of work to figure out what you'd like to do with these emotions and desires. Only you will know when it's time to start sorting this stuff out. But when it is time, be sure to listen to yourself and keep an eye on the promises you've made to yourself and to God.

In the meantime, there will be lots of things to sort out. You'll be dealing with new emotions, ideas, thoughts, ways of acting, and things you'll want to do. And in the end, cultural stereotypes shouldn't guide your reaction to this stuff. They're just too limited. They won't give you a good guide to all the things you might feel, or all the things you might face. Each girl is different, and each girl's sexuality is hers alone. So, listen to God to understand just what kind of woman you're becoming.

FRIENDS

We're into what our friends are into. This is totally true during our teenage years. After all, think about where or how you met most of your friends. You probably met while participating in school council, playing on a sports team, or going to the same church. If so, you won't find it too hard to imagine that hobbies aren't the only thing friends have in common. Most friends believe a lot of the same stuff, act the same way, and have similar life experiences.

It's not too crazy to imagine that friends might have similar beliefs about their bodies and about sexuality. In fact, it's simple: friendships influence your views about sex and sexuality. Your friends will play a huge role in how you think about the world and yourself.

This is a big deal to admit to yourself if you're just discovering your interest in guys. You're bound to have a ton of questions about what's going on, so it's really important that you hang with a group of friends that can be helpful to you. You need to find a group of girls that have the same morals, ethics, and values that you do about sex and your body. This is the only way to be sure you can talk about what's going on in your body and make good choices about what you want to do and what's comfortable, instead of just following the crowd.

Sex

For Christians, talking about sex can be hard. But it can also be easy. The easy part comes because the answer to sex should be no until you're married. Christian girls (and guys) are expected to keep their bodies pure for the spouse that they'll marry someday. So, it can almost feel un-Christian to have a whole bunch of super-specific questions about sex, especially if you're not supposed to be having it anyway until you get married. But the truth is, asking questions about sex isn't the same thing as having sex. And it doesn't mean that you're wanting to have sex, either. Knowing what's what in sex is about education, not about breaking your vow to God and your body.

So what's the hard part about sex talk for Christians? Well, the flat-out truth is that sex isn't *always* something that happens after you're married. The real truth is that some Christian teenagers end up having sex before they're married. Sometimes, the answer doesn't end up being no when Christian girls (and guys) are faced with sexual temptation. And if these girls and guys haven't asked that many questions about sex before, or they don't know very much about the realities and risks of sex, it can make things even worse.

Who falls right in between the Christian who keeps herself pure and the Christian who ends up having sex? It's the girls and guys who want to touch, make out, cuddle, or be close to one another. This is probably the biggest group that Christian teens fall into. And even though there won't be any sex involved, knowing the risks of going too far is important—it's the only way to keep making good decisions as you grow into womanhood.

The rest of this chapter will cover all sorts of sex questions, from the health risks of sex to questions about homosexuality to worries about pregnancy. We'll also get a look at how sex works, what it's for, and the personal side of sex: how it feels to be aroused, and what to do if you think you've gone too far or are worried you might.

Q: **Why is keeping my body pure such a big deal in Christianity? No other girls seem like they even have to worry about it.**

A: You're right. Girls who aren't religious don't worry as much about keeping their minds and bodies pure. And you know why? Reason number one is that these girls aren't in a relationship already, like you are. You know . . . that relationship you're in with Jesus? Ya, well, that makes the whole purity thing a big deal for us Christian girls. Paul basically gives it to us straight in 1 Corinthians 6, letting us know that our bodies aren't our own. They are temples, and we've promised them to Jesus. So, purity becomes a big deal because everything we do with our bodies says something about the way we're treating God's temple, which is meant to stay pure and follow his design.

Three more reasons to stay pure before marriage:

Commitment. This is the number one, big-time deal for Christian girls and the act of sex. The New Testament sums this up pretty good when the apostle Paul says that if people are going to be interested in sex (but also be interested in Christ), then they've got to marry the two things, literally. He told Christians that sex should happen between married people. Otherwise, it will be impossible to keep an eye and a heart toward God's will.

Honesty. You won't even enjoy sex if you don't have honesty between the two of you, and the most complete honesty comes in a marriage relationship. Having a committed partner, a husband, makes speaking up easier.

Safety. For girls who have sex outside of marriage, safety is the biggest thing that burdens their minds. What if they get pregnant? What if their guy dumps them? What if their parents, pastor, or friends find out? What if, what if, what if? For girls having sex inside of marriage, they're doing something that won't get them in trouble. They're doing something good for them that they don't have to hide, stress out about, or keep bottled up inside.

Q: Can we just start at the beginning and go over the basics of sex?

A: First of all, sex is not something you should be embarrassed to ask your parents or other trusted adults about. I know, I know, it's a bit awkward. But it's really important that someone you know and trust gives you the information you need. Second, this isn't premarital counseling—so I'm not going to go into every detail. But here are the basics:

First things first—the names. Vagina and penis. (Say these words a few times if you're still cracking up right now. Go ahead, get the giggles out, and I'll catch you back here in five.)

God designed a man's and a woman's bodies to fit together for the purposes of pleasure and procreation (a big word for having kids). A man can fit his penis into a woman's vagina, and his semen (which you'll learn about in the chapter on guys) is released into her body. This feels really great for both the husband and wife.

When this semen meets up with a woman's egg, a baby is created. No birth control is 100 percent perfect—so whenever you have sex, there's a chance you could get pregnant. This is one of the reasons it's important to keep sex inside a marriage. Another, more important reason is that God's design for our lives is to only have sex with the person we're married to.

Q: Kids at my school are so into sex. Sometimes it makes me feel like I should be, too, even though I know I've promised to wait. Would it be that big a deal if I broke my promise?

A: The pressure to have sex can be overwhelming for girls. It's like you want to have a boyfriend, but you feel like sex has become a part of the whole "dating package."

When you're up against this kind of pressure, having a heart for God and keeping your body for marriage can seem like a choice nobody's making anymore. But that's not true. More than half of all teens are keeping their virginity, and you should too.

The best reason to keep your virginity is God. Not the Bible, but God himself. Sure, the Bible might have a lot of passages that deal with lust, fornication (sex between people who aren't married), and sin, but God isn't a bunch of words. You and God have a relationship. Like a promise you've made to a friend, God expects you to be cool with what you and he have agreed to. He counts on you, just like you count on him.

Another good reason to keep your promise to virginity is you. That's right: Y-O-U. Your body is the only one you've got. It's a gift from God. In fact, it's one of the biggest gifts God gave you. Why would you want to give something like this to some guy you met a few months or even a few years ago? You've had the gift since you were born—it's not worth handing over to someone you've only known for a little bit of time.

The last reason to keep your promise to virginity is health-related. My advice on sex and health is this: sex means two people's bodily fluids will mix. If one person has a sexually transmitted disease, he can spread sickness, infection, or just plain *dirty*-ness to the other. You could also end up pregnant, and I don't know too many teenage girls who are down with being moms when they're fifteen years old.

So teen sex just isn't a great idea. Your promise to virginity is important for yourself and for your relationship with

God. But it's also the smart girl's choice for keeping her body healthy.

Q: Guys at my school are always joking about masturbating. Is it bad for you or a sin? Is it something girls do too?

A: This is one of those questions Christians have all sorts of different opinions about. Some people think it's okay to touch your genitals until you reach a sexual climax. Other people think that Christians should skip it because it just doesn't lead to purity. Most often we hear about masturbation when people are talking about boys. What you hear less about are girls who masturbate. But this doesn't mean it isn't happening.

Usually when girls or guys get sexually excited, they start to think about lustful things. They imagine nudity, sex, or other fantasies to make the experience more enjoyable. This is where the big Christian debate comes in. Some Christians argue that masturbating messes with the purity of your mind. They argue that purity is a two-part package: body and brain. So, masturbating leaves our bodies pure but not our minds. When you're committed to purity, masturbation becomes a big hurdle to cross. But some people argue that it's healthy for you to get that physical release. If it's something you're thinking about, talk to an older Christian who you trust.

Q: It seems like I'm the only one who doesn't really think it's okay for girls and guys to be homosexual and have sex with the same gender. Am I the only one who thinks being gay isn't God's plan for sex?

A: No, you're not alone. In many religions, the majority of believers don't think homosexual (same-sex) relationships are appropriate. But yes, you are in the minority today if you're just talking about what you'll hear on TV or at school. Most talks you'll hear about sexual education in public schools will stress that homosexuality and heterosexuality are both okay options for you.

Most Christians don't live by what they hear in school or society, though. Christians live by God's Word as it appears in the Bible. Though the Word doesn't say anything about rejecting, being mean to, or thinking less about people who are in same-sex relationships, it does say a lot about girls and guys who want to have sex with someone of the same gender. Specifically, almost all Christians interpret the Bible to say it's a "no go"—under God's design, sex is something for one guy and one girl only. Not two guys, and not two girls.

Q: My boyfriend and I are both Christians, but we can't keep our hands off each other. What other stuff can Christians fool around with besides sex?

A: You know the truth as well as I do: there's a ton of "almost sex" that happens between teenage Christian couples. Even if no one tells each other directly, there's always gossip about who got together with whom, or how far this or that person went with somebody.

What is in the Bible, though, is one main theme: purity. From the way we act to the way we think, it's stressed over and over again that God designed us to serve him and to stay pure. That means our bodies as well as our minds.

When we consider that, it means that getting physical with a guy isn't always the best choice. The question here is like saying, "How much can I get away with and still be cool with God?" That can lead to things you are uncomfortable with. You might feel bad, guilty, or burdened by what you've done. You might feel like you need to hide it, or that God is mad at you. So, while it's unrealistic to tell you to keep your hands off each other and never even kiss, it's also worth warning you that getting physical will get confusing when you're not emotionally ready to go further—i.e., get married.

The best thing you can do with a guy is listen to your heart and take the advice of Christian adults that you trust. Don't just follow others—what you do with your body is between you and God, first. Then it's between you and your boyfriend.

Q: I have a friend who keeps having sex and getting together with different guys. I worry she's going to get sick or something. What could happen to her, and how can I help?

A: Great question. It's a good idea to be concerned if you know someone like this. Sex is serious business health-wise because people are exchanging fluids. There's a good chance of spreading or contracting a disease if you're not careful. Here are some of the most common diseases people can get:

Diseases	Herpes (her-pees)	Syphilis (sif-a-less)	Chlamydia (cla-mid-e-ah)	HIV-AIDS
What it is:	It's a bit like a cold sore and forms around the mouth or genitals. An extreme kind occupies nerve centers in the spinal column.	Bacteria that get into the bloodstream and causes people to have rashes and sores.	Bacteria that get into and infect a person's genitals.	A viral infection that lives in a person's body, permanently.
What it does:	Causes blister-like sores that may be itchy or break open and ooze. They last from seven to fourteen days.	Syphilis lingers in a person's body and causes breakouts of rashes, fevers, or sores. It eventually breaks down vital organs.	Chlamydia damages the urinary tract and reproductive organs.	AIDS lives inside a person's blood system. It breaks down the immune system so the body cannot fight disease.

How you can get it:	Oral sex with an infected person or genital contact with an open, active herpes sore.	Oral sex with an infected person or genital contact with an open sore.	Oral sex or genital contact with an infected person. Skin-to-skin contact at the point of infection.	Oral sex or genital contact with an infected person. Also, fluid exchanges, like blood and breast milk.
What it can do:	Herpes can't kill you, but it can make your life a big pain. The biggest risk is having children, because herpes might infect the baby during delivery.	Syphilis can kill you through brain damage or vital organ failure. In the meantime, you become a carrier of the disease and run the risk of infecting others.	Untreated, chlamydia can lead to Pelvic Inflammatory Disease (PID), which may cause infertility.	AIDS will kill you; it's as simple as that. It destroys a person's immune system, so the body ends up being too weak to fight off diseases.

So these are some of the more than 240 sexually transmitted diseases (STDs) that your friend risks contracting if she keeps sleeping around. But if she still isn't convinced by the risks and refuses to stop, the least she can do is protect herself. Condoms are an easy way to cut down on STDs, but they're not 100 percent effective. There's still a chance she will get one of these (or other) diseases.

But remember, you're not in charge of anyone's sexuality except for your own. Don't enable your friend to keep engaging in risky sexual behavior by always bailing her out. Don't feel bad if you have to ask an adult for help in a situation like this. I know this sounds like the last idea you might consider when it comes to sex, but I'm serious: ask someone who's older and who's cool. They'll be able to help you out, and she would much rather know on the front end than find out later when someone's got a fatal disease.

Q: My boyfriend and I started having sex. We knew it wasn't right, though, and we felt totally ashamed. We asked God to forgive us and haven't had sex since. But now I think I'm pregnant. How can I tell? What should I do?

A: If you've had sexual intercourse (with or without a condom), you could have become pregnant. There's no exception to this rule. Whether you had sex one time or ten, you could have gotten pregnant. If you've skipped your period since you last had sex (gone more than one month without starting again), you should take a pregnancy test immediately. Even though you might be scared about what you'll find out, taking care of a new baby growing inside you is a big responsibility. Waiting only hurts the baby—it's not worth it.

After you take the test you have two options. Okay, I lied. Really, in my opinion, you only have one option, no matter what the test says: tell an adult you trust.

Why? Because talking about what happened will be good for you. If the test ends up being negative, telling somebody about it is a great way to begin an accountability relationship. Try connecting with an older girl who can guide you and help you keep your promise to yourself not to have sex again.

If the test is positive, it's even more important to tell an adult. Adults can get you the support you need if you're pregnant. You'll need doctor exams, medical care, love, support, and probably even a shoulder to cry on from time to time. Also, if you have an adult there to support you, it may keep you from making choices that you may later regret, like having an abortion.

If you don't think you can tell a parent, try telling a support agency. Many Christian support agencies can help you carry a baby to term and then offer your child a safe, loving, adoptive home if you can't raise the child yourself. Here are a few resources that can offer you a choice like this and guide you from there:

> Hope's Promise: 1-303-660-0277; online at:
> http://www.hopespromise.com
> Liberty Godparent Home: 1-888-760-5433; online at:
> http://www.godparent.org

You can also go ahead and break the news to someone you trust at your church, if that's more comfortable for you. Sometimes when people who aren't your parents hear your big news first, you can get a better idea about how people are going to react to what you have to say. This can be good practice for telling your parents. Also, a church member you trust probably already knows your family and can help you find a way to tell them.

Eventually, though, you're going to have to break the news to your parents. I won't kid you: this will be really tough. They'll be glad that you told them, but first they'll probably be shocked. This means that they might blow up and get angry. Or it might mean that they'll spaz out or get hysterical. There's always a chance that they'll take it really well. Just know that in the end, it will work out all right. God won't be mad at you. You will have fun again. And it won't be the end of the world.

Chapter 11

Guys—What's Up with Them?

Guys can be total freaks. Seriously, the way guys act during their teenage years can sometimes leave you scratching your head and thinking . . . *what*?

But take pity on the boys, ladies. After all, guys are going through most of the same stuff you are right now. It can be a lot for them to handle. How much? you ask. Well, find out for yourself by checking out this chapter. Here we'll spill the 411 on how much boys are having to deal with and just what's going on with their bodies and minds.

About the Outside

The physical changes are the biggest thing that you'll probably notice when a boy your age starts maturing. He'll start having a wispy little mustache. His body will start to smell more powerful, or maybe unpleasant. His face might break out in zits. He'll shoot up three, four, five or more inches just over one summer break. His voice will crack and then deepen, and his overall body will get bigger, or more muscular.

With all this stuff going on with the outside of a guy, there's a good chance that you can spot which boys are in the maturing process. Here's what you can expect for each kind of change you see:

Height

Ever wonder why guys are so much shorter than girls? Even into high school, some guys seem to just lag behind the girls in terms of inches. It's like they haven't grown up, literally. Height is one place where it's pretty obvious that boys lag behind. It's a scientific fact that girls are first to have their growth spurts. Boys come second.

Girls can sprout up and get some good height starting as young as age eleven. But boys have to wait a few years. Most don't start gaining inches until they're thirteen or fourteen. This means that there may be a big gap in height between you and the guys all the way from sixth grade until you both get into high school.

Be sensitive about this, if you can. No guy goes home from school psyched that the girl he likes is seven inches taller than him. In American culture, boys are still pictured as taller and more muscular than girls, so as boys are working on becoming men, being the shorty of the pack isn't such a great feeling. Not only is it obvious they lack height, but a guy can feel insecure because of the way men are pictured in the media, or because of the teasing he gets from friends and other people in his life.

Don't think guys don't worry about it. They do.

Hair

The first sign of hair you might be able to spot on a guy's body is facial hair or armpit hair. His leg hair also begins to become thicker, darker, or curlier, but the big giveaway is usually a little mustache. Growing this body hair is a slow, subtle process for guys. It's not like he's going to go home one day with a baby face and show up the next morning on campus looking like Ashton Kutcher.

It's the same deal when it comes to the armpits, chest, legs, or other parts of a guy. Some guys end up being so hairy that their friends nickname them after everybody's favorite huge, fuzzy Wookie in *Star Wars*, Chewbacca. Other guys end up with less hair than a newborn baby. It's all genetics in the end. A boy will usually end up looking as hairy (or not) as other people in his family.

Either way, what a boy decides to do about his body hair is a personal choice. Most guys do one of two things: begin shaping it, like wearing a goatee on their faces, or begin shaving it, like getting rid of hair that grows on their backs or other parts of their bodies.

ODOR

Unfortunately for them (and you, sometimes), the same hormones that turn boys into men can cause the transition time to be really smelly. Boys have glands (just like you) that tend to produce a strong-smelling sweat during puberty. Add this to a nice round of basketball on the courts, or a game of football after school, and you're in for one ripe-smelling boy.

Most boys know this, though. It's not like guys walk around thinking, *Do I smell manly, or what?! You know you love it!* No way. They're typically just as embarrassed as you are when they stink. And just like you, there's not too much they can do about it, other than using deodorant, snagging a clean change of clothes, and getting themselves into the shower every day. It's just something boys have to learn to manage.

SKIN

His skin is just like yours. Both of you are struggling to come up with clear complexions. Nobody wants to be a pimple-face ... not now, not ever. Just like your skin, his skin will be clear if his facial pores stay unclogged. If they don't, then bring on the zits. Same goes for the rest of his body. Clear pores mean no pimples.

Sometimes boys can struggle more than girls do with pimples. Guys usually have more skin to deal with (they're taller and usually bigger), and they also have to deal with things like tight football uniforms that trap sweat, dirt, and bacteria on their skin. This can really clog up a guy's pores. Plus, they don't get the benefit of wearing concealer and makeup to hide their imperfections.

His routine for clearing up his skin is exactly the same as yours: keep his hands off and his skin clean. If he picks or pops pimples, he'll end up with the same result too: acne scars. So guys and girls are a lot alike when it comes to skin.

BODY

Okay, girls. We're just going to launch into what the big deal is with boys during the teenage years: the penis. The truth is, it's just another part of the body, like an arm or a leg. However, it's the male sex organ, and that sometimes makes people giggle.

Here's the deal: boys who have reached maturity are able to have an erection (a hard penis). When the penis gets hard, it's because a big dose of blood gets sent there. An erect (hard) penis is a sign that a boy's body has matured to a point where he can have sexual intercourse and is capable of reproduction.

Being capable of reproduction means that his testicles are able to produce *semen* (sea-men), a milky fluid. Semen is basically a liquid that's got tons and tons of tiny reproductive cells (called "sperm") in it. His testicles produce the sperm, and they are released through the penis. When a boy has reached maturity, this sperm becomes available.

But for boys, it's not like all this happens overnight. All the parts we talked about—the penis, the semen, the testicles—and a whole bunch of other stuff in his body have to go through pretty big changes before a boy reaches maturity.

This can whack him out. His body is producing hormones that are shooting all over. Some of the hormones make parts of his body grow bigger, some parts get more hair, and some parts develop more muscles. In short, his body is working overtime. Every bit of his body (inside and out) is turned up to 100 percent.

Having all their body parts working overtime can tend to make boys act a bit weird. (Like you can't relate, though?) For both guys and girls, maturing means letting your body take control from the inside out. Your body is reorganizing and making changes on the inside that will eventually show up on the outside.

About the Inside

If you think you can be an emotional wreck from time to time, don't think it's just a girl thing. No matter how many times you hear guys say stuff like, "Girls are so emotional!" or, "Girls are more in touch with their feelings," it's just not true. Every teenage guy who's ever been on the planet Earth has gone through the same emotional ups and downs that you're going through. The big problem for boys is usually finding an outlet for these feelings.

In many cultures, including America, boys are supposed to be strong. They should be brave. They should be leaders. They should be smart, capable, and able to figure their way into a good job and the ability to support a family someday.

Big Myth: Guys don't understand what girls are going through.

Real Deal: Guys do understand. They're going through the same stuff.

But where in these requirements does it say that it's okay for guys to be sad? Where does it say that it's fine for a guy to cry in public, to throw a hissy fit, or to get bummed after a breakup? The answer is: nowhere. And this can be tough on boys. Even though they're going through a lot of the same feelings you are, they don't have a way to let these feelings out. If they do, they worry that other people will think they are dorks or just can't hack it as men.

This is the farthest thing from the truth. Guys who have the same emotions as girls when they're growing up can hack it as men. In fact, guys who feel comfortable letting all their feelings out—not just the feelings that are usually associated with guys—often make the most well-balanced adults. That's because these guys understand that most people are coming from the same place.

A guy who already realizes this is a rarity, though, during the teenage years. Instead, most boys are caught up in the whirlwind of trying to be somebody. This means boys can act like real jerks sometimes—like when they're trying to prove they're cool, manly, or no longer a little kid. Or, it can happen when guys feel like their friends want them to be one way, their parents want them to be another, and you or other girls expect something totally different.

Because of all this confusion, some guys push all of their feelings inside. It's not that guys are trying to hide their feelings; that's not the point. What's usually going on is that they're still learning how to communicate all the stuff they're feeling inside. They don't want stuff to slip out that might not be cool, manly, or "what a guy would do."

When boys look around at what's cool in culture, how their friends act from day-to-day, and what they see around them in their families, they might feel overwhelmed. Their minds, bodies, souls, and lives are being overhauled during their teenage years, and it's all a guy can do to try to keep up.

Big Myth: Being a Christian means having to go against cultural norms.

Real Deal: Being a Christian means getting to go with Christ's norms.

EMOTIONS

So, a guy might realize all this change is going on but not know what to make of it. He might not know how to act in response. If so, there's a good chance that he'll keep his feelings inside. He may hide crushes. He may pretend he's not sad. He may go along with the crowd, never speaking up for his own likes and dislikes. Or he may end up acting rude—lots of guys tease and make fun of people because they don't know what else to do, or how else to act.

When a guy does this, he can turn into a real jerk. But from his perspective, if he can keep all the confusion inside, no one will ever know that he doesn't have all the answers. No one will know that he doesn't really know what's going on, or that he's scared, confused, sad, or frustrated about stuff. By keeping stuff inside, a guy is able to live up to the pressure he might feel around him to be strong, keep his head above water, be smart, and figure his life out.

Big Myth: Guys don't talk about how they feel.

Real Deal: Some guys don't know how to talk about how they feel.

Guys aren't a mystery. In fact, they're a lot like you. You'll be surprised at how similar some of our emotions are. If you can understand this, you may be on track to understand guys a little bit better and figure out why it's sometimes hard for boys to say what they really mean or act how they really feel.

Chapter 12

Your Rights

The first thing any girl should know about herself is that she's strong, capable, and worth every bit as much as anybody else on the planet. Girls aren't "second best." They never have been, and they never will be. But this doesn't mean that girls are number one either. It doesn't mean the world revolves around girls or should cater to their needs. It shouldn't mean that girls get extra advantages, special treatment, or an easier ride through life than guys do.

What a girl should know is that she's equal. Not better. Not worse. But worth the same as every person, because we're all God's creations. We're all human beings who want to preserve our health, protect our rights, and experience what life has to offer without the fear of danger, harm, or discrimination.

Unfortunately, this isn't always possible. Some girls have to struggle against a world that unleashes violence and harm against them. Hard times can come in an instant, and girls can find themselves in over their heads. And all this can be confusing, scary, and frustrating.

Girls do have a voice, though. They can speak up when their rights—or their bodies—have been violated. We can also get active and put a foot down against things that push too far or have injured us in some way.

But learning how to get a vibe like this can take some time.

Because girls who stick up for themselves or speak their mind are sometimes considered bossy or rude, lots of girls say, "No thanks" to sticking up for their rights. They don't want to look like jerks, and they don't want people to think they're mean.

Or a girl can be embarrassed about sticking up for herself when something horrible, like rape, has happened. She might worry that people will think it's her fault. She just might not want to cause a big scene because then she'd have to talk about it. And really, she'd just rather forget.

The Rights We've Got

Two rights that all girls have at their fingertips are safety and free speech. The power of these two rights can do wonders for us. They mean we don't have to keep quiet about stuff that's happened to us.

SAFETY

Where It's Ours: At school and in our daily lives in the town or city where we live.

How We Get It: At school, your right to education is also a right to safety. Because you can't learn if you're being bullied, it's the school's job to protect your personal rights. For girls, though, we should know that our right to safety also means a right to sexual safety at school.

Being bullied isn't just about getting your rear end kicked on the playground. It's about boys who touch you when you don't ask them to. It's about teachers who make sexual jokes in front of you, or even about you. It's about the taunting, yelling, and verbal assaults—like a guy yelling, "Whoa, babies! . . . Jog those jugs over this way, sweetie," when you and your girlfriend run during gym class.

A girl's right to physical and mental safety is a regular and very public problem when it comes to sexual harassment. But just because it's a big deal doesn't mean there's nothing you can do about it. And, it doesn't mean that it's okay for guys to act like this. Sexual harassment can spark a mental meltdown. You might rack your brain trying to figure out why it's happening to you. Is it because of the way you dress? Is it the way you act, or something you said?

You know what—don't even go there with yourself. The way another person acts toward you is his own choice. It's as simple as that. Don't even think twice about turning people who are sexually harassing you in to a teacher you think is cool, a counselor, or some other adult. In the meantime, go ahead and get yourself out of harm's way. Leave and/or alter your schedule so you don't end up being at the same place at the same time as the people who harass you.

Being protected from physical and sexual abuse in your town is another story. There, your physical safety is protected by law. Murder, violence, and acts of abuse—like rape—against all people are illegal. If this kind of crime happens to you, the attackers can be taken to court and sent packing to jail.

Free Speech

Where It's Ours: Everywhere. Well, except at your house. I'm not even gonna mess with your mama here, and neither should you! But in general, your constitutional right to voice your opinion or your concern applies anyplace you go. Whether you're at school, the mall, the beach, or working out at the gym, your thoughts are yours to express.

When it comes to a girl who needs to speak up because her rights have been violated, free speech guarantees that she won't be shut down. Her voice has just as much right as anyone's to fill the air. And if she's been violated, it's her right to voice these concerns out loud, and in public.

How We Get It: Free speech is ours, just for living in America. But you have to speak up to exercise your right. Speaking up can be the most difficult part for girls who've had terrible things happen to them. It's like if they say something, then everyone will know. Everyone will stare at them. And everyone will ask questions. But being able to walk into a room and finally blurt out what happened is something that many girls can't ever do.

It's a privilege to be able to speak up and defend ourselves. Living in an era where girls don't have to silence themselves is a blessing. So speaking out is something unique and something you can do to stick up for yourself and stay safe. However, if you're uncomfortable talking about something that has happened to you—tell someone close to you who can become your spokesperson about this while you work it out inside your heart and head.

The Gift of Fear

Sitting around one day after high school, I was watching Oprah. I saw her guest talking about why girls end up getting their rights violated because of their inability to say no.

I kind of like to think of myself as pretty independent. So, when I saw the girls on the show, I figured they couldn't be that much like me. But then I watched and watched as girl after girl said a lot of the same things I did when they were being pressured by situations that were uncomfortable. Instead of sticking up for themselves, the girls backed down because they didn't want to be rude.

It was like these girls didn't know how to say, "Go away," "Leave me alone," or "No" when they were being put in uncomfortable situations by other people. The girls were more worried about being nice, cool, or not being rude than they were about that little feeling inside of them that was telling them to "watch out—this isn't safe."

This little feeling is our intuition, and it's the first thing we can use to know where being nice should end and our rights should begin. *The Gift of Fear*, by Gavin DeBecker, scared the you-know-what out of me when I read it. But his main message made me think.

If I keep ignoring my little feelings of fear and danger because I don't want to seem rude to somebody, I'm eventually going to put myself in a bad situation. His book convinced me that fear lets us know that we're probably headed into a dangerous situation. When we feel fear creeping up inside, that should be our signal to hightail it out of there, pronto.

Your rights are about protection for you. When you feel that little twinge of fear, it's a sign you need to listen up. You need to focus on that feeling of fear, analyze the situation, and, if necessary, speak out, say no, and get yourself to a safer place. You've got to assert your right to protect yourself.

Staying Safe

Another thing you can do to protect yourself in a dangerous situation is learn to fight back. Girls don't often think about something terrible happening to them, but bad things do happen. Girls get beat up, raped, burglarized, battered, and abused. It's not pretty, but it's real. It can happen to you, and you shouldn't kid yourself about this.

Getting a strategy locked in your mind for times of trouble is a great idea. It doesn't matter if you're online or IRL (in real life); knowing a bit about self-defense and smart thinking can cut down your chances of being at the wrong place at the wrong time.

SELF-DEFENSE IRL

1. Get Your Body Out of Harm's Way. Try to skip the stairwell if you're by yourself. Lots of stairwells lock behind you, leaving a girl pretty well trapped from the inside. Because stairwells don't get a lot of traffic, potential attackers could use the stairwell to find their victims.

Same goes for other places that don't get a lot of traffic,

like alleys or tunnels. Get yourself into a place where your body is around other bodies. This will minimize your chances of being attacked, just because you aren't by yourself.

2. Carry Protection on Your Key Chain. There's a number of sprays on the market today designed to keep girls safe. One of the most popular choices is a small can of pepper spray. In an emergency you can flip the guard back, spray your attacker, and make a run for safety or cover. Cans of pepper spray are about ten bucks apiece.

3. Get the Heck Out of There. Remember to listen to your own sense of fear. Being rude isn't as big a deal as being attacked. If you're feeling freaked out by someone or something, do whatever it takes to get away, even if you have to be a jerk about it. This goes for boyfriends, guys you've never met, girls that want to brawl at parties, or anyone else who's scaring you.

4. Try a Self-Defense Class. Some of these classes will teach you martial arts for self-defense. Other classes will focus on getting your mind and body in shape for an emergency, so you can be calm and have a better chance of getting away if an attack happens to you. Check your local community listings for these kinds of classes. Also, most college campuses offer free self-defense classes that you and a crew of girls can drop in on for free.

SELF-DEFENSE ONLINE

1. Don't Agree to Meet People IRL . . . Ever! Worry about meeting people in your own neck of the woods before you try to hook up with some guy named "pimpjuice2709" who lives in some other state. It's not that everybody online is a freak or anything; it's just that there's no way to know who's who and what's what with online chat.

2. Don't Give Out Personal Information . . . Ever! Where you live, what your phone number is, and where you go to school are all things you want to keep to yourself. It's a basic move of self-defense that will keep you safe from a potential stalker, attacker, or a general creep. Don't kid yourself about people like this not being out there online. They're there. So be careful, and keep your lips sealed about personal stuff.

3. **Do Log Off or Put People That Seem Dangerous on Your Ban or Block Lists.** Self-defense is about keeping the most distance between you and the people you think may end up hurting you. Take action right when you get that little creepy feeling. If something about somebody doesn't sit right, ditch him by disappearing. Or, shut off his access to your e-mail or IM lists by blocking him.

4. **Check your Facebook and MySpace settings to make sure your profile can only be seen by your friends.** Be careful about what information you post and who is allowed to see it. If they're not private, pictures from Facebook and information like your address or school can end up on search engines where anyone can find it.

SMART THINKING IRL

1. **Walk, Park, or Stand in Well-Lit, Public Places.** (My policeman father is going to be so proud!) Though it would be nice to be able to just do as we please in the world, girls can't. We are targets for people who want to do us harm, like kidnappers or rapists. We're also usually lighter, not as strong, and have less ability to do serious damage to a bigger person who tries to attack us. So be alert. Don't put yourself in a place that will make it easier for someone who wants to harm you. Stay out in sight and near as much light as you can to be sure you're seen.

2. **Get the Word Out on Your Whereabouts.** It may seem like a freedom to head out the door and never tell a soul where you're off to, but it's actually really important that people know where you are. Always tell your parents where you're going. Call in if you change locations. And give people around you a heads-up on what you're doing too. Telling people stuff like, "Hey, I need to crash for the night, so I'm headed home" lets

them know where you should be and when. If you go missing, they can get the word out sooner that you may have run into trouble.

3. Plan Ahead. When one of my girlfriends was attacked and robbed, I was shocked at first. But then she told me when and where the attack had taken place, and my shock turned to anger. I was so upset that my friend could have been so careless. She and her boyfriend had walked home right through one of the most violent parts of town in the middle of the night.

It's not that I haven't done dumb stuff like that too. I have. But the attack really made me mad because it seemed like something she could have prevented by planning ahead. It seemed like something that could have happened to me if I didn't plan ahead too. What's real, though, is that my friend couldn't have done anything about being attacked. Sure, she didn't plan well and put herself in a potentially bad situation, but it wasn't like she was asking to be robbed. She happened to be at the wrong place at the wrong time.

While a girl can never guarantee she won't end up in a situation like my friend, she can get smart and always plan ahead. For all parties and nights out when you know you'll be out late or in a part of town you're not too familiar with, know what's going on with your transportation. Don't head out onto the street at, like, two in the morning and try to hoof it across a part of town that you're not familiar with. Don't catch a ride with a stranger. Don't rely on the bus system to get you back home when it's late at night.

Smart Thinking Online

1. Stay Anonymous. There's a reason we have screen names online, and it's not because they're so cute. The digital world is a place of make-believe. We can be whoever we want, just by making up a name for ourselves. This means you're never going to be sure whom you're talking to when you're chatting to people on IM. For safety's sake, keep this illusion up on your side too. Skip telling people in chat rooms details about yourself, like your age, weight, race, hair, eye color, hometown, or your real name.

Anyone legit will want to chat about other stuff that's interesting to you both, not about who you are or what you look like.

2. Don't Believe Everything You Hear. The Web (I hope you know) is full of junk. The Web is also full of killer stuff that's totally worthwhile in a girl's life. But because it's hard to tell the difference, you have to give up on getting the absolute truth online when it comes to people. There's no telling if they are really who they say they are on the Web. There's no way to test for phonies, liars, or fakes. Keep your brain set to "maybe" when you're on the Web. After all, what you're reading and talking to people about *may be* true, but it *may be* a big bunch of bull.

Violations of Your Rights

The end of this chapter brings us to the hard part: rape, assault, attacks, or other abuses against girls. These are the worst and most intimate kind of violations against your personal rights. The attacks can be brutal, and many girls carry the effects of the attack in their minds for a long, long time.

The first thing to say about girls in this kind of situation is that you have to be honest with what has happened to you. If you've been forced to have sexual intercourse against your will, you've been raped. If you've been beaten or sexually abused in some way, you've been attacked. It did happen, and you shouldn't try to pretend it didn't by ignoring it.

When something like this happens to you, the truth has to come out. It's my absolute and sincerest hope for every girl who reads this book to believe that being raped or attacked isn't something she should hide. It's not her fault, even if she feels embarrassed about what happened.

What's real is that the attack wasn't your fault. It wasn't something that God did to punish you. And it's just something that you're going to have to grow from because you won't be able to make it go away. If you have to, repeat these three things to yourself again and again: "It's not my fault, I'm not being punished by God, and I'm going to have to get help and grow from it." Until you believe this stuff, you won't begin to heal from what happened to you. You'll be too busy racking your brain with questions when a lot of those questions just don't have any answers.

Big Myth: Guys are just jerks. I'll just deal with their joking about my body.

Real Deal: Guys are abusing your rights if they tease you about your body.

Instead of racking your brain like this, there's a better option: talk, counseling, prayer, and love. Embrace your right to free speech and tell someone exactly what happened to you. This can help you heal, but it can help other girls too. The more we know about how girls are attacked or raped, the more we can do to get advice out that will keep girls safe.

Please, please, be sure to speak up. Connect with an adult you trust or a counselor at your school, talk to someone from your church, or call the police. After you've spoken up, keep your eyes on the people who can help you most. Watch them for direction, and let them guide you through the grief, sorrow, or frustration you might feel. Also, try to keep your heart toward God. The real truth is that there are no easy answers about why bad things happen to good people. Worrying about solving this mystery is a wasted effort. God doesn't use stuff like rape or attacks to punish us.

Big Myth: Girls are supposed to be polite.

Real Deal: Girls are supposed to protect themselves. Speak up if your rights are being abused.

And last, keep your heart open to love. Give in when people want you to cry on their shoulders. Take people up on their offer to talk about things. Doing things like this will get you out of your own head and build back some of the trust that may have been lost after you were attacked. Love won't solve everything, but it's an essential part of getting your body, mind, and soul looking like the girl you used to recognize.

Here's a list of places you can contact to start down that road:

RAPE and ASSAULT

RAINN (The Rape, Abuse & Incest National Network): 1-800-656-HOPE; online at: http://www.rainn.org/

Campus Outreach Services; online at: http://www.campusoutreachservices.com/

KIDNAPPING and ASSAULT

NCMEC (National Center for Missing and Exploited Children): 1-800-THE-LOST; online at: http://www.missingkids.com/

Part three:
SOUL

Chapter 13

Family

Right now, as I write this chapter, I'm sitting pretty among the clouds while my airplane jets toward the West Coast and the ocean-side city of San Diego. My weekend is booked with family parties, celebrations, and gatherings, all in order to cheer on my cousin as she graduates from college.

Here's the funny part, though. I don't even know my cousin that well. We're a couple of years apart in age. She lives in one state. I live in another. And overall, we don't really talk that often.

So why put out the cash to hop a plane to her graduation? Because it's a "family thing," that's why. We may not hang out on a regular basis, but the support we offer each other—like showing up at graduations or weddings or other big events— is one part of who we are. It's one part of why people in my family know they're loved unconditionally.

No matter the time we spend apart, no matter the things we don't know about each other, at the very bottom level we know we can count on the family (or, as we call it, the "fam") to be a cheering section throughout our life. Members of the fam will always be there in a pinch. They never shy away from showing up just to show their love. And usually—in my family, at least—you can count on the fam to go above and beyond when it comes to loving you through embarrassment.

Big Myth: My family is whack!

Real Deal: All families are whack; that's what makes 'em real.

For example, in my family nobody even thought twice before yelling stuff like, "Woo-hoo! . . . We love you, Kate-a-ma-wait-a-ma-ding-dong! Go, go, go!!!!!" while I was running down the soccer field to score a goal. They'd yell it even if all my friends were there. They'd yell it even if the guy I had a crush on was there. They'd yell it even if I turned bright red and just wanted to die, right there on the spot. It was all good in my family. And it was all a part of being loved.

Of course, this doesn't mean family time is always filled with puppies and daisies and cotton candy and soft, fuzzy bunnies. The truth is, family life is hard. Your sisters and brothers can be big freaks. You can act like a spaz. Your mom can be overbearing or bossy. Your dad can be too strict, or not show you the amount of love you really need.

Over the long haul, you'll probably find that members of your family are a source of strength, but this knowledge will be hard-won. You'll have to endure fights, gossip, feuds, breakdowns, splits, divorce, and possibly even terrible things like abuse. You'll be asked to keep secrets. You'll be asked to take sides. You'll be asked to be brave. You'll be asked to compromise. You'll be asked to sacrifice. You'll have to pull the weight of family members from time to time when the going gets tough for one person or another.

And you know what? Sometimes you'll feel like all this stuff isn't fair. You'll feel like it's too much, that it's not your deal, and that you'd rather die than face another day the way things are currently going.

In one case, you've got good times, unconditional love,

and family support. In the other case, you've got hard times and the potential for feeling frustration, pain, and even a lot of anger.

Families are always changing emotionally. Sometimes you're high. Other times you're low, so get ready to open up a piece of your soul and learn about family life. Get ready to learn how you can listen to, look at, and love your family in order to create a better, stronger you as you grow into womanhood.

Family Flux

A quick look at the television families that are on-screen nowadays gives us a clear picture of what family flux is all about. On one end of the spectrum there's the show *Brothers and Sisters*. Between the five Walker siblings there are working moms and stay-at-home moms, families with kids and without kids, and a whole bunch of drama in between.

On the other end of the spectrum, take a show like *Hannah Montana*. It features a single dad and his two kids who are always fighting or competing with each other. We're told that the mom died when they were little, and the only time we see her is when Miley sees her in dreams and stuff. Otherwise it's just the three of them dealing with real life and fame all at once.

Then we have other shows like *Smallville* that feature kids who are being raised by adoptive parents, or aunts and uncles. The only similarity that ties all these shows together is that they're all hits. And it's no wonder. Each show is about different stuff, but the families in the shows are real. They give a glimpse of the different kinds of family structures that are out there and show how real life doesn't always look the same from family to family.

Families come in all shapes and sizes. In the United States, divorce has split many families and reorganized them when parents got remarried or lived with new people. In other cultures, like Asia or the Middle East, families can include parents as well as grandparents and other relatives too. So when we try to say what a "normal" family is, there's just no good answer. Family structures are changing all the time, depending on lots of different factors.

Here are four good guides to go by for figuring out what makes a family:

A FAMILY IS A SUPPORT SYSTEM, A CHEERING SECTION, AND A SAFETY NET

This is why close friends, people from our church, or other people we know and love are sometimes called "our family," or "sister," or "brother."

A FAMILY HAS SOMEONE IN CHARGE

It might not be a mom or dad all the time, though. It may be an aunt, a grandmother, or even an older sibling. Either way, a family usually has at least one person who guides, cares for, protects, and raises the others.

A FAMILY IS ABOUT CARE, PROTECTION, AND CONCERN

It's not about looks, beliefs, or hobbies. Family is about the deep stuff. Do we care unconditionally about other people? Do we love and want to protect other people? If so, things like what people look like or what they like to spend their time doing become less important.

A FAMILY RESPECTS YOUR SPACE

Even in a family where people get along and treat each other great, people need room to find themselves. People need space to grow. For girls, we often need privacy, a place to let our feelings out, and the ability to take time for ourselves. It's important for us girls to have a place to get away, even if we have great families.

The Good

This is the easy part. Good times in our families are the one thing people are most likely to record. For example, think about where your family keeps photos in your house.

Now that you're on track and thinking about your family's photo collections, this is what I want you to do: pick yourself up, grab this book, and head off to the nearest place in your house that has photos of people from your family. I'll wait here while you hoof it over there. . . .

Okay, now that you're looking at some photos, focus on one of them and remember why or when it was taken. Then go ahead and give your memory a little jog to bring bits of that day, event, or time in your family's life back to you.

Whatcha come up with? A party? A vacation? A wedding, graduation, or birthday? Either way, there's about a 99 percent chance that whatever event you came up with was one of joy for your family.

That's because photos are all about our best moments. You don't wander around someone's house and find yourself surrounded by a ton of family pictures that feature bummed-out faces. Imagine that for a minute. What if you looked around the corner to find a cute little frame with the word *love* written around it, only to see a picture of a mom and her daughter hanging at the beach, glaring at one another with looks of annoyance?

Even if you can imagine a photo like this, and might even have a whole bunch of them in your family, did you ever see one of them up in a frame? Did you ever see a picture like this scrapbooked into an album with a cute caption on the side that says something like: "Bring it, Mom! . . . Kelly gives Mom the evil eye because she's still mad that Mom busted her for ditching school last week!" Please! Most families just don't go there. Ever.

Instead, almost all families like to get all snapshotty about events that bring the family together in moments of joy, support, love, fun, and friendship. These are the good times, and most families like to record them. Why? Because the pictures record the best of our families: the inspiration, the love, the support, care, and nurture.

Family Emotions	Inspiration	Love	Support	Nurture
What It's All About:	This is the feeling your family gets when you support one another. This support can lead you to feel unstoppable, and your confidence makes your family burst with pride.	Love is the feeling you get when you go all-in for someone: you've got their back, and you dream with them to help them be their best.	Support is a result of the listening, encouragement, devotion, and belief you've given to your relationships with others.	Nurture is the cuddly stuff. Physical nurturing is stuff like doing favors or giving hugs. Emotional nurturing is stuff like always being there no matter what.
Why It Matters:	We need to make strides toward bigger and better things and look to one another for growth. Without inspiration, you'd have no one to take along on the journey.	Love causes your soul to grow. Without it, you can begin to feel hopeless about all sorts of things in life.	Support is what assures you that you won't stop short of goals that would make you a better person. It's your direction and compass for those times when you're lost.	Nurturing gives you that sense that everything is going to be okay. It leads to feeling like you'll always land on your feet.

| Managing It: | To make the most of inspiration, be alert to people's strengths and weaknesses in your family. You'll see the best in each member. | Generate love from the little things to the big. Be sure people in your family encourage one another. This is a surefire way to generate love on all sides of the equation. | The key to support is to strike a balance and to iden- tify where (and when) people need support and where and when you can give support to others. | Nurturing can some- times be a one-way street. Be sure no one is always on the receiving end of the care. When family members give care in return, they'll be surprised how much deeper their souls will feel. |

The Bad

The bad times in your family can range from little fights between a brother and sister to full-on family battles. Some- times the bad times tear families apart for a small period of time. Other times, what's gone bad can tear a family apart for good.

It doesn't seem like people would want this, but the truth is that bad times are hard to talk about. Getting through these bad times can be even harder. That's usually why families don't spend Christmas dinner bringing up the laundry list of who did what to whom and who's at fault for what. This is stuff that families try to keep on the downlow. But act- ing like this is the absolute worst, and I'll tell you why. If we can't express how we feel about the rough spots in our family life, we're likely to become quiet, secretive, and hold grudges against other people. Ever been there?

If members of your family don't have a way to say what

they feel or confront one another when problems come up, the bad times will only get worse. When people are trying to hide or push their negative feelings down, everything becomes tense and uncomfortable.

Sure, fighting and getting your feelings out can be really uncomfortable, too, but fights come to an end. At some point you've said what you feel, and the others have too. The people involved may still be mad or hold a grudge, but at least nobody is carrying around all their feelings in secret.

The moral of the story? Bad times in families are only made worse when people act like everything is fine.

Family Emotions	Guilt	Anxiety	Suspicion	Anger
What It's All About:	Guilt is a kind of regret. Usually you feel guilt when you know you've done something wrong. It can nag you long-term and be an ongoing problem.	Anxiety is the result of worrying that you're doing the wrong thing. It's a nervous feeling that can cause you to feel insecure and lead to self-doubt.	Every family has to deal with keeping secrets, things they're not proud of. When trust is in question, suspicion can lower the level of safety you feel in your family.	Some families struggle with forceful anger like yelling, violence, or abuse. Others struggle with hidden anger, like resentment, hatred, or disapproval.

Why It Matters:	Guilt can show you where you've gone wrong. But you may feel guilty when you've done nothing wrong. This is the "guilt trip" that families sometimes put on each other.	Anxiety can paralyze you. Constant worry about what to do can leave you power-less. It's important to be sure anxiety doesn't leave you without your own voice about your future and your role in the family.	Suspicion cripples trust among family members. Lines of commu-nication can break down—or they stop altogether. Without a way to com-municate, families start to unravel.	Anger is the quick-est way to make the bad times in your family worse. Once this occurs, it's hard to calm back down. Finding a grounded place to reopen lines of commu-nication can be difficult, and grudges may develop.
Managing It:	Guilt has to be man-aged by your mind and actions. Figure out whether or not the guilty feeling is justified. Then work to confront things that need to change.	When you feel anxious, you're feel-ing your own brain working on overdrive to imagine the worst. So it's important that you stop what you're doing and chill. Breathing techniques can increase calm and bring you back to a clear, cool head.	Managing suspicion is hard to do. Once a family member has blown another person's trust, it's pretty hard to give that person another chance. But you have to strike a balance and work toward rebuilding trust.	Anger is manage-able, no matter what anyone tells you. People have control over how they react and can take a step back when things get close to the breaking point.

The Ugly

Now we turn to the hard part: abuse and dysfunction. Though all families have their share of fights or poor communication, some families have a dynamic that is absolutely broken—through abuse, physical violence, or sexually inappropriate behavior.

If you're in a family that's physically or sexually abusive, it can be frightening. When people constantly fear they'll be hit, struck, beaten, physically punished, or touched in sexually inappropriate ways, their bodies and minds are almost always tense. It's a nervous feeling in the pit of your stomach, and it never goes away.

Most people in this situation live in absolute fear all the time. They fear that they'll be abused. They fear for other members of the family who are being abused. And they fear that people outside the family will find out what's going on. Abuse is almost always a big secret.

Because of this, people who finally speak up or tell on family members who are abusing them have a hard road ahead. I'm just going to be honest about this because it's true: when you report abuse in your family, it can sometimes make things worse. But (and this is important) if things do get worse, it will only be for a short time. In the long run, the only way your body and soul will be free from someone who is abusing you is to speak up.

What you might wonder if you're in an abusive family is, *Why me?* Unfortunately, girl, there's no good answer to this one. There are a lot of things that we don't know about God or about how the world works. If I tried to give you a quickie answer, I'd just be lying to you. What we do know is that we have to trust God to make good on his promises to work all things for good in our lives.

You're not alone if you're in an abusive family. When the United States Department of Health and Human Services added up all the cases of abused kids in 2001, they found out that almost 13 kids out of every 1,000 were abused. This means that at an average high school, there might be 25 or 26 kids walking the halls each day who live in abusive homes. If you spread that number out over freshmen, sophomore, junior, and senior classes, it means that seven or eight people in your class may be abused.

But even though all of these people who are being abused are just kids, it doesn't mean that they can't get help. They can. One thing we know for sure is that all kinds of people are able to overcome difficult times. This might not be any consolation right now, but it's something you should never forget. You're the only boss of you, and you're the one who can change your life for the better. And though you will be scared, sad, and worried about making waves if you try to speak up about your abusive family (or other situation), the real deal is that worry is wasted and useless. When you're being abused, it's more important to seek help, immediately. The sooner you can get yourself—or whoever is being abused—out of the situation, the better.

This might mean some seriously tough choices, though. You may have to give up living with a parent. You may have to move to another city, state, or even country. You may have to change schools. And you may have to make all new friends and start over fresh. What you *won't* have to do is keep living with abuse. This is a trade that's definitely worth it.

So how do you go about speaking up once you know you've got to get help?

TELL AN ADULT THAT YOU TRUST

A good way to get your voice heard, without having to do something scary like call the police, is to tell a teacher. If you tell a teacher at your school, s/he is required to report it. A trusted teacher can be the ultimate lifeline if you're in a situation where you or another family member is being abused.

Big Myth: I'm betraying my family if I speak up about abuse.

Real Deal: You're betraying yourself and your future if you keep quiet.

When word gets out that an abuser lives in your family, help will come soon. Unfortunately, the city or town you live in is usually in charge of getting this help to you, and they can sometimes be slow about doing it. But don't let that stop you. Don't give up if it takes a few tries to let someone know about your situation, especially if you're the one who has to speak up for a little brother, sister, or even a parent. You've got to keep your mind calm and know that you're capable of getting help in this situation.

Get in Touch with Local Centers That Help People in Your Situation

Look in the phone book yellow pages under titles like "social services" or "human services" for numbers in your area that might be able to help. You'll have to talk to a grown-up on the phone, but they'll be super-nice and go as slow as you need them to. And because you can call these people from any phone, usually at any time of day, it means you can plan to get yourself to a safe place when you call.

Contact a Hotline

If you can't find the phone book, or have trouble locating help near you, try any of these hotlines:

The National Child Abuse Hotline: 1-800-422-4453

All of these calls are free, so you can dial the numbers anywhere. When you do call, the people who answer the phone will listen and give you ideas about what to do next.

ABUSE *IS* AN EMERGENCY—DIAL 911

If you live in a family where fights regularly get so out of control that people begin to throw punches or objects at each other, you can call the police. All you have to tell them is the address of your house. Then police officers will respond and look into what is going on. If you do this, you'll have to talk on the phone, and you might also have to talk to the police officers once they get to your house.

Try to pick one of these four options and go with it. You don't want to take on the problem yourself. Hitting or being violent in return will only make things worse. Running away or escaping from the problem by doing drugs or drinking will only make things worse. And frankly, you're worth more than this. You deserve a great shot at life, and you shouldn't shy away from making that shot yours by speaking up. Get help and get on with your life, unafraid.

Chapter 14

Friends

"Hey!" Nadia yelled down the hall after her best friend, Ally.

Looking back over her shoulder, Ally stopped in her tracks. "Hey . . . what's happenin'?"

"I was looking for you everywhere," said Nadia. "When I was in the bathroom this morning. I guess they didn't see that I was in there, because I totally saw Maddie in there talking trash about you to Casey."

Ally's smile turned to a tight scowl after hearing this. "Maddie was trashing me to Casey? . . . She's such a backstabber!"

"You know she is," said Nadia. "Remember when she spent the night at your house and was like 'Ally, you're *soooo* one of my best friends,' and then the next day she blabbed all the stuff you told her to everybody? It wasn't even funny like Maddie said it was. I don't even think she was doing it as a joke, no matter what she says."

"Ugh! Why does she have to be like that?" said Ally, angry and hurt. "I totally like her, but she always ends up being a gossip queen and a jerk whenever you tell her anything. As if I'd want to keep telling her stuff . . . hello?!"

Nadia felt for Ally. She tried to support her by giving Ally the 411 from what she overheard in the bathroom.

"Trust me, Ally, Maddie doesn't even care about your feelings. In the bathroom she was agreeing with, like, everything Casey said, even when Casey said she thought you were lame and didn't know why in the world Maddie would hang out with you. She's so two-faced!" Nadia insisted.

"It's like Maddie just wants to be popular no matter what, you know?" Ally said in a frustrated way. "She just blabs everything she hears and agrees with everyone who she thinks will get her more friends."

"You know that part of it is that Casey is friends with Dustin and Zack," Nadia said.

"You're probably right . . . Maddie's been into Zack since day one, remember? Even when I told Maddie at that party that I really liked him, she's totally been flirting with him and trying to find ways to get into his little crew of friends," Ally told Nadia.

"I think that's why Maddie was trashing you," said Nadia. "She probably thinks that if Casey likes her, then she's going to be able to get Zack to like her too. You know what I mean. Like, if Casey thinks Maddie is cool, then Zack will, too, because Casey and Zack are friends, right?"

Ally was bummed. "Whatever . . . Maybe so. It's just so dumb, though. Why does Maddie have to be like that?"

That's What Friends Are For?

If you've ever heard a discussion like this before, you know that it's the worst. Substitute your friends' names for Ally, Nadia, Casey, and Maddie, and you're probably able to flash back to a similar time in your life with your friends.

These kinds of situations are confusing, to say the least. But because part of being a girl is learning how to get a group of friends that's true, builds us up, and cheers us on instead of backstabbing or tearing us down, we have to ride out the ups and downs of different friendship relationships.

Here's the deal. During your teenage years, you need friends beyond belief. Friends keep you centered, share your dreams, encourage you to reach your goals, give you an outlet for your problems, and help to make the good times even better. Friends can be there when your family situation isn't the best. Friends can investigate questions with you, help you grow, and give you good advice. Your best friends make you better in some ways. Friends who can see into one another's souls and care about growth, support, and the future of each other are the kind you really need.

But there's no guarantee when it comes to friends. Not everybody is like, "How cool are you?! Let's be friends forever!" The fact is, you won't bond with everyone, and it's no big deal. There are different kinds of friends, and you'll need some of each. So don't sweat it if you don't become best friends with everyone that comes into your life.

The Hobby-Friend

Hobby-friends are people we end up meeting because we revolve in similar circles. The hobby-friend is someone who plays the same sport that we do, a person we can hang with every weekend at church, or a girl or guy that works at our jobs.

There's good and bad parts about having hobby-friends. The good stuff is that you don't usually expect to have it out with a hobby-friend or have to endure full-on fights. The fact is that we just don't really see hobby-friends often enough to move to a deeper level where we're each pushing each other's buttons or making one another mad.

Here's the thing, though. Our hobby-friends aren't the shoulder we cry on when things go bad. Our hobby-friend doesn't usually have to deal with us when we're cranky, stressed, bossy, or being a big jerk. Instead, hobby-friends almost always get to see us at our best because we spend only a limited amount of time with them. And guess what? We usually see their best side, too. It's hard to guess what our hobby-friends can really be like day in and day out because we both see each other for so little time.

There's always an exception to any rule, though, right? In the case of hobby-friends, the exception might be a hobby that crosses over into your daily life. You guys might see each other in all your classes, go on trips to performances or games, and see each other at weekly practice sessions.

Big Myth: Friendships should last forever.

Real Deal: Some friendships last only until an event or project is over.

What all of this time together can mean is that you have a chance to do some serious bonding. Be on the lookout for hobby-friends that can cross over into your daily life. You may pick up a tried-and-true friend.

THE PSEUDO-STALKER FRIEND

Ever have a person who follows your every move? This can be the absolute worst. It's like you're being stalked. Go to your locker, and that person is there. Sit down for lunch, and guess who sits next to you? Make your way to the bus, and guess who's right in back of you in line? It's like you can't get away from the person. It's like she just can't take the hint that you don't really want to be her friend. Help!

If this has happened to you, chances are that you've spent just about a million hours or so dreading that you'll bump into her. It's a good bet that you make an intentional effort to avoid her. You may even have figured out how to alter your daily routine so it's harder for you and this person to connect . . . ever.

If you have a relationship that has come to this, you've got to just be brave and take the situation head-on. Here's why: both of you deserve better.

Think about it from the other person's side first. Every minute this person spends following you around is a minute she could be spending building a friendship with someone who really clicks with her.

So here's the hard part about knowing this. Someone has to tell your pseudo-friend this truth. (Hint, hint . . . that someone is you.) Don't feel bad if you're just not feeling that buddy-buddy vibe from someone who hangs around you. God has designed every person as an individual. This means that some individuals won't like the design of other individuals, and vice versa. Does this mean any individual design is bad, lame, or not worth being friends with? Nope. But, it does mean that each design is going to be appreciated by some people, and not by others.

Life can get lonely. When people don't know where they fit, sometimes having someone—anyone—to click with can feel like a lifeline.

If this kind of person has latched onto you, be gentle but honest. Try to find resources around you (either people or events or clubs) that the other person might be really interested in.

THE TRIED-AND-TRUE FRIEND

Pop quiz: Can you ask your best friend the following questions and actually get an honest answer?

1. Do people think I'm fat?
2. What do I hope to become or do in the future with my life?
3. What is best about the person I am?
4. Am I annoying sometimes?

The four questions here represent the four kinds of knowledge that our very best, very deepest, most intimate friendships should have.

The first question asks something superficial, or about the surface stuff in our lives that people see every day. Can your friend hit you with the honest truth?

The second question asks about our minds, hearts, and souls. It's a personal question that probably not everyone who knows you could answer. It's a question that wraps up what you're all about or what you dream you'll be all about in the future.

The third question is about inspiration and respect between people. Does your friend look at you and see a pretty face? Or, does your friend look at you and see charity, honesty, intelligence, or a kind soul?

Big Myth: Friendships are all about cliques.

Real Deal: Friendship is all about companionship.

The fourth, and last, question is about the good and bad of your relationship together. Is your friend someone who can look with honesty at the kind of relationship you have with each other? If so, the answer to the question should be "yes." All people are annoying at some time or another to everyone. Even the very best friends have times when they think, *Go away! You're bugging me to death!*

If you and your friend can talk honestly about all four of these things, it's a good bet that you're tried-and-true friends.

A tried-and-true friend is absolutely important. In fact, it's something that you can't (and shouldn't) live without. Why? Because deep friendships turn us into deep people from the inside out.

Here's how all this works. When we chill with people we don't know that well, our souls don't grow. Instead, we just talk about casual stuff like movies, boys, girls, gossip, classes, or other superficial stuff. But these aren't exactly topics that are going to expand our minds. They just aren't enough to help us understand what we really care about in our souls.

Big Myth: Everyone should be your friend.

Real Deal: Not everyone clicks with everyone else.

Having casual friends like this is fine. We don't have to become deep thinkers or spend time philosophizing about the world with every friendship we make. But we should be sure that our very best friends challenge us to do this.

With our best friends, we need to have the ability to vent about what's hardest in our lives. We also need to have a relationship where we can get some advice. We all need someone who's got our back, good times or bad.

Casual friends just can't do this for us. Only a tried-and-true friend can help us do this. So remember these four things that make a friend tried-and-true:

1. Truthfulness about what we hear and see around us in life.
2. An ear to listen to each other's dreams and know what's in the other person's soul.
3. An eye to find what's inspiring within the other person.
4. The openness to be able to come clean with how you really feel about the other person.

Guy-Girl Friendships

"Are you guys going out or something? What's the deal?!"

"Oh, we're just friends, you know."

Ever heard this before? Me too. In fact, I've even been the one trying to convince my friends that I wasn't into a guy I was hanging out with. Here's the lame part too: I actually thought they believed me!

The world of guy-girl friendships is an absolute land mine during your teenage years. But this doesn't mean you shouldn't have guy friends—not at all. It's just that having guy friends comes with the potential for some confusing stuff.

Guy-girl friendships can head one of two places. They can lead nowhere in terms of romance and you two can just hang as friends, or your relationship can head into romance. The real deal is that guys and girls like each other. Duh. Whether we're thirteen or seventeen, there's a good chance that we've got our eye on a guy we like and are hoping to have some kind of relationship with him. And the potential for the two of you to stay "just friends" is there.

But let's take the second option here and imagine that a guy-girl friendship is heading toward romance. Falling for a guy you're close to is a totally natural reaction. Almost every girl I know, including myself, fell for one of their guy friends at one time or another. And truth be told, most of the guys I know fell for at least one of the girls they hung out with too. It happens to both girls and guys.

Here's the deal. Mental and physical desire for romance is all around you during your teen years. That's because you're becoming more aware of the sexual side of your body and mind. It's like you want to be around certain guys almost all the time, you can't stop thinking about them, or they can't stop thinking about you.

When guys and girls move in the same circles, get to be close friends, and spend a lot of time together, it's natural to want to give more of yourself to one another. It's exactly these kinds of feelings that blast a relationship off to a great start. And when couples start off as friends first, a solid foundation is usually created. Because friendship takes longer to develop, going out with a friend can feel safe and secure.

Where guy-girl friendships begin getting sticky is when

the friendship doesn't explode into deeper feelings that *both* people share. If you're a girl who has a whole bunch of guy friends, you can almost count on this happening to you at least once in your life. Either one of the guys will fall for you, or you'll fall for one of the guys. But it's how you deal with the situation that will determine if you can preserve the friendships you've made.

If you realize you're into him, you've basically got two choices: tell him or don't tell him.

TELLING HIM

If you go for choice number one, you risk the friendship either way. He might tell you something like, "Really, no way! I'm so into you too!" And your friendship will then become a romantic relationship.

On the flip side, he'll say something like, "Oh . . . well, um . . ." and you'll feel lame-o. Then, you'll both just have to try to move on from there. Moving on isn't always possible. Sometimes people get creeped-out when they know their friends are crushing on them and don't really want to hang out anymore. And I hate to tell you this, but sometimes when our friends get creeped-out by our crushes on them (or we get creeped-out by their crushes on us), it can turn people into pseudo-stalkers. When dissed, lots of people get obsessed with convincing the person who gave them the boot that everything's okay, or that these people shouldn't be creeped-out . . . really! "It's no big deal that I was crushing on you big-time! We should be friends like old times . . . don't you think?! Don't you agree?! I think so! Don't you?! Right . . . right . . . right?!" (Can you say s-c-a-r-y?!)

NOT TELLING HIM

If you go for choice number two, you'll just have to hang out and see if anything ever happens. This can be utterly romantic, or it can be utterly frustrating. You may wake up one day to find that you're both into each other. But you may also find stuff just stays the same. No negative change in the friendship, but nothing more than friendship develops, either. If things head this route, the friendship will get tougher, at least on your side. You'll have to live with a secret crush. So the whole time you two know each other, you'll have to figure out how to act "normal," even though you're totally sporting feelings for the guy. Keeping something like this inside can make you act differently, and it might even make him act differently, too, if he notices you're being weird or things have changed.

Big Myth: It's hard to be good friends with boys.

Real Deal: It's easy for good friendships with boys to become more.

So, What If He Likes You?

Instead of choosing a good way to act, you need to come up with a good way to react.

Boys can sometimes act like jerks when they like you. Or they can act shy, like they're not interested at all, only to make one big move when you're both alone together. So it's not always easy to figure out if one of your friends is into you.

Either way, when you find that your guy-girl friendship has grown into something more for him, try to figure out what you can do about it from your end. First and foremost, ask yourself if you want a relationship with this person. Before you make any moves that might signal that you're into him, be sure you're really interested. Dating a friend just to have somebody to go out with is usually a bad idea. Then . . .

If You Like Him Back

You've got nothin' to worry about. Like I said, a good friendship is the best basis for a dating relationship. The only downside might be the reaction you get from other friends in your same group. Or you may have to work through some issues when (or if) you two break up. If everybody wants to stay friends, having an ex-couple in the group can sometimes get uncomfortable. A great idea is to get your friends all on the same page with your relationship, whether it's just starting up or it's on its way to splitsville. Be honest with everybody involved in your lives. You'll find that eliminates most of the gossip and weirdness that sometimes go along with couples and friends.

If You Don't Like Him

You've got a few more choices to make. You could just be blunt and tell him it's a no-go between you two. This is a really hard thing to do, though. If you don't say it in quite the right way, or if he takes the news really hard, you can count on things getting ugly. And even if you say it (and he hears it) in the best possible way, there will still be a weirdness between you. This might be uncomfortable for a long time. Or it might go away rather quickly. Only time and the kind of personalities you both have can tell.

Secret Side of Friendship

Girls don't usually have it out on the playground. It's not often that you see girls throwing elbows and blows out in the quad. And girls aren't known for being physically aggressive.

But girls are mentally aggressive. Any girl who's been caught between two warring girlfriends can vouch that this is true. The dirty looks, the intentional snubs, the snotty voices or looks, and the teasing and trashing that go on behind girls' backs is rough stuff. It's every bit as brutal as guys are when they fistfight. It's just that it's quieter, less obvious to people around, and can go on for what seems like forever.

This is the secret side of friendship.

When a friendship goes bad, we might end up on the receiving end of attitudes like these. People do end up disliking one another. And sometimes, there's nothing we can do to fix the problem.

We can manage the problem, though. Here are three ways to keep your head above water when friendships go bad:

FORGIVE

The worst thing that can happen to a friendship that's gone bad is for people to hold grudges against each other. Think about it. Where does that get anybody? On one side, people just hold on to the sense that they're right and the other person is wrong. On the other side, people just hold on to the sense that everybody else is being stubborn and difficult.

If you haven't forgiven someone whom you're no longer friends with, try writing down why you're mad, what you think should or could have been done, how you wish things would end up, and why you're so angry. Getting all this out is the first step.

The next step is realizing that getting your feelings out is all you can do about the situation. If the friendship has gone bad, or if you're not going to be speaking to the other person any longer, there's nothing more you can do. What happened is what happened, period. Mistakes were made, people were hurt, and the friendship came to an end.

It's not the ideal situation, but it's also not the end of the world. When you can see that there's nothing else you can do about a situation that's over and done with, you'll begin to feel a weight fall off your shoulders. There's no sense in holding on to negativity. Forgive. This doesn't mean forget, but it does mean that you realize the situation has passed. Holding a grudge won't do anything but bring you anger and frustration.

Heal

Healing is the opposite of hiding. When friendships go bad, sometimes your reaction is to retreat inside yourself. This is a great short-term idea. When you're by yourself, you can listen to your feelings and figure out what's going on inside your head. But there has to be a time when you return to the world. Even if you feel sad, depressed, or damaged by a friendship that you lost, you've gotta get back out there.

Try not to write off everything you and your friend did, said, liked, or acted like as *bad* just because you two didn't make it as friends in the long run. Even though that friendship didn't last, it probably taught you something about yourself or what you enjoy. Don't let a friendship that has ended keep you from continuing with these things.

Open Your Heart

Usually when friendships go bad, you can bet that you're going to become suspicious, scared, or even paranoid about what you tell people and whom you keep around you as friends. Don't sweat this if it happens to you. You're not mean. It's natural to be cautious after a big breakup or shake-up in your circle of friends.

But you've got to shake the feeling off at some point. If you stay worried and suspicious forever, you're going to find yourself without anybody to lean on. Friends are an amazing support system, and you need them.

Big Myth: Part of being a girl is learning how to be nice.

Real Deal: Some girls act nice but are actually as mean as it can get.

To heal from a broken friendship means finding the ability to start another one even if you're scared. With every attempt you'll get better and better at knowing what kind of friend you're looking for. And with every attempt you'll get better and better at weeding out the kind of people you want to stay away from.

Chapter 15

Religion

What is religion? What does religion feel like? What about other religions? How do I find my religious center? Can religion breathe life into my soul?

Thinking about these issues is where religion starts. Each question you ask, even if you can't come up with an answer right off the bat, is a way for you to chart your own religious future. Asking yourself what you believe about religion is one way to find out what's important to you. Even better, though, is that when you think through religion to find out what's important to you, you begin to work from inside your soul.

What do I mean by working from your soul? Well, I mean that you're working from the deepest part of yourself. You're looking within to ask the questions that nag at you, that you're curious about, and that nobody else seems to be answering for you.

You're arranging what you know into your soul and shaping it to fill your heart, mind, and life with the things you believe in personally. The bottom line is that you're able to believe in religion because *you* want to.

The Dream Deal

This is the absolute dream deal when we think about religion: believing in it, living it, and letting it gel in our lives because it makes sense to us. In the ideal world, we wouldn't be religious just because everybody in our family is. We wouldn't be religious just because our parents said so.

If religion is going to play a role in your life, you've gotta make it your deal, not your parents' deal. If you've got no idea how to get this started, don't sweat it—I've got your back. You can get started by reading this chapter. Here we'll take on general questions about religion. We'll also get into why religion matters and what it can do for you when it's *your* choice, *your* life, and *your* soul that you commit to it.

Work Through These Waters

Here's the big-deal part of the chapter, where I tell you that there are many religions in the world, but they're not all the same. If you haven't heard this before in church, you probably will eventually. And it's important to know because it's true.

There are many sets of beliefs in the world. Christianity is just one of those religions. But Christianity isn't the same as other religions, and other religions aren't the same as Christianity.

How can you know this, though? Should you just take my word for it? The flat-out final answer to the last question is *NO!* Don't take my word for it. Between the big bookstores on every corner, the supersize warehouse stores that stock piles and piles of books, and your Web-searching capabilities, you can always get the 411 on your own.

Big Myth: I don't have questions because I have faith.

Real Deal: I have questions because I want to understand my faith.

Don't just take someone's word for it when you can read up on the subject yourself. Sure, asking questions is fine, but knowing it yourself is the name of the game. It's the real deal, so why not wrap your mind around it on your own?

Here are some basic differences between Christianity and other religions that will prep you for what you'll find when you dive into the info yourself:

BUDDHISM

Main Difference from Christianity: No God.

Behind Buddha: "The Buddha" is a nickname given to a prince from India named Siddhartha Gautama. When he was a young man this prince became a wandering *ascetic* (a-set-ick)—a poor, very strict student of religious knowledge—and learned tons of stuff from teachers all across Asia. Then he sat under a tree for six days and eventually figured out that there was no secret truth about the universe. Instead, the truth was that everybody had the potential to be happy. What people needed to do was escape the suffering that's caused by getting too attached to all kinds of stuff in life—like love, or cars, or money, or power. When he came to this realization, he became "awake" and picked up the name *Buddha* because of his newfound knowledge.

Basic Beliefs: Buddhists *don't* worship the Buddha; they follow the knowledge that he found and made available to everybody.

Buddhists work on keeping their minds clean, clear, and on the positive.

Buddhists hope to reach a state called *nirvana*. (You know the band called Nirvana? That's where the name comes from.) If nirvana is reached, then the suffering of life is over.

Sometimes it takes many lifetimes to reach nirvana. The energy or essence of a person is born again and again (reincarnated) until he or she reaches this state.

What You Won't Find: The community that Christians have

with God or the community of heaven. Buddhism is a very individualistic religion. It is about purifying the minds and bodies of individual people. Christians have community with their God; each person is connected to God in his or her own way. Christians also expect to meet God in heaven, to see their loved ones there, and to live in eternal happiness.

WICCA

Main Difference from Christianity: Goddess worship. The goddess is the creator of life, nature, and Earth.

Behind Wicca: Wicca originated in England during the 1950s. Some Wiccans say that the religion was around long before Christianity, but that all depends on whom you talk to. It also depends on whom you talk to if you want to know what the name *Wicca* means. Some people say it means "wise." Other people say it means "twisted." And then there's another group who think the name means "to bend or alter." Small groups of people called *covens* are the most regular way people participate in Wicca. In these groups people usually focus on ceremonies, celebrations, and rituals that have to do with people and nature.

Basic Beliefs: The threefold law—what goes around comes around. But in the Wiccan religion, what goes around comes around three times over.

Ready to get all Old English with me? The second thing most Wiccans believe in is this phrase: "An ye harm none, do what ye will." It sounds all Shakespearean, but the phrase just says that you can do whatever you want as long as you don't harm others.

Some (not all) Wiccans believe that a soul has a lot to learn in this life, but sometimes there's not time to learn it all. So a soul that still has things to learn is born again (reincarnated). When a soul learns everything it's supposed to know, it is given rest in a place called the Summerlands.

What You Won't Find: A reliance and trust in God, Jesus, or the

Holy Spirit. Christians have a relationship with God. He is our Creator, our Father, and our Mentor for life. Wiccans do not have this relationship; instead, they use ceremonies and rituals to influence their lives and the world around them. Some Wiccans try to use magic and spells to change or alter the world by calling on supernatural powers. Christians leave things up to God and work to live by his Word alone.

ISLAM

Main Difference from Christianity: Belief that Allah is God, and the Prophet Muhammad is the messenger of God.

Behind Islam: About six hundred years after the birth of Jesus, a man named Muhammad was born in the Middle East. He started out as a sheep- and goat-herder but eventually became the leader of a world religion. Muslims (moose-lems) believe that one night while Muhammad was in a cave out in the desert, the angel Gabriel appeared to him. This angel showed Muhammad some of the information that would become the foundation for the holy scripture of Islam, the Koran. The rest of the information for the Koran continued to be revealed to Muhammad by Allah (they call him Allah but believe he is the same God Christians believe in). Because Muhammad submitted to this information, the religion is called *Islam*, which means "to submit."

Basic Beliefs: Muslims *don't* worship Muhammad; he is only a messenger of God's word.

Belief in Islam means five things: you admit that Muhammad is God's last and final prophet, you pray five times daily, you donate part of your money to charity, you fast (don't eat) from sunup to sundown during a month called Ramadan, and you take a trip to a holy city called Mecca at least once in your life.

What You Won't Find: Belief in Jesus Christ as God's only Son and the Savior of the world. Islam sees Jesus as a prophet, just like Muhammad. So, just like Jesus had stuff to say that was from God, Muslims think Muhammad did too. They believe that Muhammad is the final prophet—no others will come after him. Christians disagree and think that the last of what God said directly to the world was said through Jesus Christ and the New Testament. For Christians, Jesus Christ is the Son of God and part of the Holy Trinity.

HINDUISM

Main Difference from Christianity: Tons of ways of approaching the one ultimate reality, called Brahman (bra-man).

Behind Hinduism: A really, really, really (times about fifty) long time ago, a group called the Aryans settled in the country we call Pakistan today. They brought with them their language, stories, ceremonies, celebrations, and beliefs. These practices were eventually changed and modified and tweaked until the Aryans and the people living around them came up with a kind of central tradition that was a result of all this blending. This is called Hinduism.

Basic Beliefs: Brahman is the cause and foundation of all existence. The companion to Brahman is a great goddess. She has many versions, shapes, sizes, and names.

There are also lots of versions, shapes, sizes, and names of Brahman in the universe. Some versions create, like the god Brahma. Some versions destroy, like the god Shiva. Some versions preserve, like the god Vishnu.

The universe revolves in cycles, like a wheel. A soul can be born again if it hasn't learned all that it needed to during one cycle. When a soul has learned all it needs, it is free from the cycles of the world and reaches a point called *moksha* (mock-sha).

What You Won't Find: One right path to God. For a Christian, the only way to God is through his Son (Jesus), whom you learn about in his Word (the Bible). Believing this means that we're on track to having a life with God, both on Earth and when we die and go to heaven. But Hindus do not believe in one path to reaching God. If people practice their religion with sincerity, Hindus believe that they are following one of many paths God has created for people in the world to know the truth.

Judaism

Main Difference from Christianity: Jesus is not the Messiah. He is not God's only Son or our personal Savior.

Behind Judaism: The Jewish religion is where Christianity finds its history. Here's the big difference, though: Jews and Christians believe different things about Jesus. When Jesus was on Earth, there was a big group of people who all followed God. When this group saw or heard about Jesus, some people thought he was sent directly from God and was a kind of God-man (God on Earth). People who believed this thought Jesus came from heaven so he could die as a way to make up for our sins. So, Jesus "saved" us and is called a Messiah or our Savior. These people are Christians.

Others didn't believe this. They thought that Jesus was a prophet, just like prophets from the Old Testament. When Jesus died, he was just another prophet who died, not a Savior. The people who don't think Jesus is a Savior are called Jews. They are still waiting for God to send a Messiah.

Basic Beliefs: Saying the Sh'ma (shhh-ma): "Hear O Israel, the Lord our God, the Lord is One."

Big Myth: All religions teach the same stuff.

Real Deal: All religions teach specific stuff.

Orthodox Jews are the strictest. You might remember seeing an Orthodox Jew because the men wear very particular outfits. They have black hats, grow beards, and let two strands of hair dangle out each side of their hats and curl into little twists. Orthodox Jews follow all of the Ten Commandments and the 613 mitzvoth (mits-va), or rules, God gave to Jews in the Old Testament.

Conservative Jews are pretty traditional too. They do some of the mitzvoth and keep the commandments.

Reform Jews are the most relaxed and mix modern culture with Judaism.

What You Won't Find: Jesus Christ as a personal Savior. Do you remember when you committed your life to Christ? You might have prayed for Jesus to come into your heart at a youth retreat, at church, or even just one day when you were by yourself. Either way, you asked Jesus to be your Savior so you could have a relationship with him. Jews don't believe that Jesus was a Savior, so they don't ask to have a relationship with him. Instead, they're committed only to God.

Compare What You've Got

If Christianity is one religion, why are there Catholic, Protestant, and Orthodox Christians? The short answer to the question is that the world has lots of versions of Christianity because there are lots of kinds of people. It's important to remember that the various Christian denominations agree on more issues than they disagree on. But we don't all read information and get the exact same message from it. We don't all come to the exact same conclusion after thinking about stuff. So basically, the reason for all the different versions of Christianity is that people are different. They each read the Bible, but they each come to different conclusions about what the words of the Bible mean for their daily lives.

If you're not comfortable in your current church home, or are just interested in other options, visit some other places of worship with your family. Read up on the order of worship for Catholics, Baptists, Presbyterians, Methodists . . . and the list goes on. See which aspects of the Christian faith are really *you*.

Whether you go to a Protestant, Catholic, or Orthodox church, if you've asked Christ to be your savior, you're a Christian.

Come Out Clean

When we know what other religions believe, it's easier for us to see where we want to plant our feet. When we know what kind of Christianity we believe in, it's easier to see where we stand. It's important to know both of these things if we're going to determine just where we've planted our feet in the world of religion.

Knowing where to plant your feet is important if you want to make your faith your own. How important? Really, really important. Why? Because knowing just where you stand is the only way you can start taking steps forward. If you don't know where you've planted your feet, it's hard to understand how other religions compare to your Christian faith. If you're unable to blaze your own path ahead, or just don't know what's out there, you'll be stuck taking baby steps the whole way.

Baby steps are fine, I guess—if you're a baby. But you're so past that in your life now. Think about it. With everything else, you're psyched to put in your two cents, have your say, and make your own choices. When people keep us from being able to get a word in edgewise on a subject, it can even make us mad. So why would we want to let religion be the one thing where we just take itty-bitty steps that someone else says are okay?

Being Christian can feel amazing and can become a deep part of your soul, but only when you make it your own. Your steps forward, your stumbles, bobbles, and falls are the only way to grow into womanhood with a mature faith. You won't always take the best steps forward, but they'll be *your* steps. Because the steps are yours (not your parents' or friends'), they will translate into personal, immediate, and meaningful growth for your soul.

Here are four quick ideas on how to take your own steps to finding soulful religion, for better or worse (but probably better because you're the bomb, and that's what being you is all about!):

1. ONLINE COMMUNITIES

If you're going to be IM-ing people all night anyway, why not make them Christian people from around the globe? It's a safe bet that you see what Christianity is doing near you all the time. But what is Christianity doing for people who live in places like Africa or Latin America? Did you know that people are converting to Christianity like mad on those two continents? Find out why and see what religion is doing around the globe in the lives of others.

24-7 Prayer; online at: http://www.24-7prayer.com
ChristianChat; online at: http://www.christianchat.co.uk

2. SOCIAL SERVICE GROUP

See what your Christian faith looks like outside the church. Getting connected with people who aren't specifically Christian can give you a better idea of how your faith looks to others and what kind of an impact faith makes outside Christian circles. This is the part of Christianity where you let your actions speak louder than your words. Give a project your all, and see how your faith can help you and others get stuff done in the world.

3. "ALONE" VACATIONS

The summer youth group trip is a *must* for many Christian teens, but what about kicking it on your own? Seriously . . . just you, a Bible, the music you love, and a few hours all by yourself. Isolate yourself to see what lies within. Spend the day just hanging out and feeling the vibe of your soul when it's just you and the love of God.

4. Concert Circuit

Festivals are a dime a dozen these days. This means music, art, and entertainment are probably just a few minutes or hours away. Check up on lists of Christian festivals that are rolling through your town to get in touch with a wider group of teens than you're used to seeing. Fresh faces mean fresh inspiration, fresh connections, and fresh ways of seeing Christ in your life and the world around you.

Cornerstone Festival; online at:
http://www.cornerstonefestival.com
Ichthus Festival; online at: http://www.ichthus.org

Stay Committed to Your Dream

So let's say you've heard me loud and clear. You're all about being proactive and getting religion to make sense for you, personally. You've checked out other faiths. You've gotten busy looking into what kind of Christianity you'd like to practice.

But what then? Should you feel any different? Will religion be any more real to you now?

Want the real answer to these questions, nice and short? If so, then here it is: you probably won't feel any different right off the bat.

You know how in movies there's sometimes a scene where a person has one of those "aha!" moments? It's like everything just sort of changes for the person and they begin to see life really clearly. They walk differently. They talk differently. Their whole life takes a turn for the better, and things are just about perfect.

You know this isn't real, right? It's cool, but it's totally fake. And so are people who act like this. The real deal is that change takes time. When you shift toward filling your own soul with the information you really want to know about religion, it's gonna take a while to sink in. Your life won't be changed overnight. Your life won't become dramatically different. Mostly, you'll just begin to feel more together. The pieces of the world around you will click a little bit faster. And probably, you'll even find that you're interested in new stuff and excited about learning more.

If you feel like this, you're on the right track. It's a sign that your soul is becoming big-time. Big-time independent. Big-time whole and complete. Big-time into a religion that matters to you, personally. And what all this means is that you're in the process of making religion real for you.

Making religion real is just about the most important thing you can work on during your teen years. If you're way into religion right now, you may need to pull back and find a way to make your faith long-term, not just a temporary blazing spark. If you're religioned-out right now, be honest about feeling like this too.

When religion works in a person's life, it's usually something they do for good. So, if you're at one extreme or another—or you don't quite know where you stand—take as much time as you need to figure it out. Otherwise, you'll grow into womanhood with all these shoulda-coulda-woulda kinda questions that never get answered. You'll be carrying around a religion that's either too confusing to be worth it, too much like a chore you do for your parents, or too much like a trendy flavor-of-the-moment kind of fad. In the end, religion like this gets tossed aside.

So to make religion stick, make it yours. Get serious about your soul and see what questions lie in there. Don't shy away from asking about these things, because growing into womanhood means creating a soul that's purely you. It means creating a Christian life that is yours, personally. It means creating a kind of religion that lasts. It means learning how to shape your soul and learning how to shape your life to match.

Chapter 16

Lending a Hand

A soul is an empty thing without service. You know why? Because God made us for relationships. First, our soul was designed to thrive on being committed to others who help us to grow and find our creative center. Second, our soul thrives on giving something inspiring back to others.

People call giving something back *volunteering*, but the real deal is that it should just be called *life*. Offering a part of yourself in service is something you should do just because you're a human being—not because you're trying to be nice.

You see, nothing's equal in the world. No matter how much work, effort, and energy you put into making everything fair for everyone, it just doesn't end up that way. There will always be a baby who ends up without parents. There will always be people who go hungry. There will always be people who are rich, healthy, and safe, while other people are poor, ill, and in danger.

This situation is summed up in one sentence flat in the Bible: the poor will always be with us. If we take the word *poor* and apply it to the world we live in, there's a lot of things that we could use it for. People may be financially poor, have poor health, experience emotional poverty like loneliness, or end up without anything inside them spiritually.

So what's a girl to do? Well, you've basically got two choices:

Choice #1: Do Nothing

You may have heard this argument before as one reason people don't need to worry about helping out: the Bible says the poor will always be with us. People come up with arguments like, "No matter what I do, it won't really make any difference. I know giving is a part of building relationships and a part of my soul, but it's better if I just focus on my relationship with Christ. Through prayer and his will, things will be made right in the world."

Choice #2: Do Something

On the other hand, some people use the same argument from a different perspective: the Bible says the poor will always be with us. But it doesn't say, "The poor will always be with us . . . so you know what? Why don't you not worry about helping. I'll figure it out." These people don't put up excuses but instead say stuff like, "So maybe I can't change the world—big deal. I can lend a hand if somebody's always going to be in need of help. I can change one life."

I bet you can already guess that I won't be recommending choice number one. Nope. No way, no how. The world is a gift to us from God, and one way to develop your soul is to plug in and lend a hand. After all, lots of girls don't even give helping out a second thought. We get so busy with our own lives that we end up forgetting other people. That's why it's so important for girls to sit down and give the idea of service some thought.

Complete the following sentences. Then match your answers to the list of opportunities in this chapter where you can make a difference.

"Souled on Service" Quiz

During the week I have _____ hours where I'm really not doing that much, other than chilling.

When I get really into something, it's usually got me working: indoors | outdoors

I'm better at using my: brains/smarts | body/strength

I like working with other people when it's: a big group | one-on-one

I burn about _____ bucks a week on movies, food, CDs, and other stuff that's just for fun.

Tap into Your Neighborhood

Set your soul on serving people who live right next door. Here's a list of needs that people you know might have:

ERRANDS

What's It All About? Elderly people and single moms often end up needing some extra help with things.

How Many Hours Does It Take? One to two hours, whenever it's convenient for the person you're helping.

What Will I Do? Some people can use your help to do errands, clean around the house, cook meals, and get yard work or small construction jobs done.

Whom Will I Work With? The person you're helping, and maybe a friend or two if you bring someone along.

Can Money Help Out? No. Serving the elderly in your community is just about getting to know them and giving a hand with their daily routine.

Community Service

What's It All About? From keeping your neighborhood pool clean to helping out at the library, there are a lot of places to plug in that will help your community.

How Many Hours Does It Take? One to two hours. Whether you have to put these hours in on a regular basis will depend on what you've committed to doing. For example, volunteering to help out at the library may require you to be there at the same time each week. But if you're just doing a community cleanup day, you'll only have to schedule yourself to be there every so often.

What Will I Do? All sorts of stuff. You might garden, babysit for a neighbor, clean up trash, check out books, or just keep an eye on things.

Whom Will I Work With? The couple of adults who are responsible for whatever project you've decided to work on. Depending on who else has said yes to pitching in, you also might end up getting to work with teens your age too.

Can Money Help Out? No. Community service is all about pitching in to make the neighborhoods we live in better. Nothing can do that except effort.

Tap into Your Church

Set your soul on serving people at your church. Here's a list of needs churches are always looking to meet:

Child Care

What's It All About? During service each week, most churches have a nursery for young children and babies. A nursery can always use an extra hand, especially if you go to a big or busy church.

How Many Hours Does It Take? One to three hours, once a week.

What Will I Do? Cuddle babies, help feed and change their diapers, and play with young kids.

Whom Will I Work With? Some adults, but mostly groups of kids and babies.

Can Money Help Out? No. Giving your service to the nursery is all about showing up and giving kids your heart.

Service Setup

What's It All About? Churches usually need people to man the doors, breezeway, courtyard, and service tables every week, for every service that happens during the day.

How Many Hours Does It Take? One to two hours, weekly.

What Will I Do? All sorts of things. You might greet people, hand out programs and bulletins, direct traffic, organize fliers and handouts, or man the coffee table.

Whom Will I Work With? A few different adults, mostly. Regular church volunteers or staff members will be in charge of coordinating everything. But you'll probably also bump into other teens, like yourself, who are pitching in to lend a hand.

Can Money Help Out? No. Your church will be in charge of getting all the supplies. You just need to show up and go with the flow so you can help where they need you most.

Tap into Society

Set your soul on serving people who live in the community around you. Here's a list of social needs in almost every town:

Homelessness

What's It All About? People end up without a home for many reasons. Sometimes it's single adults. Sometimes it's a family—kids can be homeless too.

How Many Hours Does It Take? As little as one to two hours per week, anytime you can swing it. Offering your time to an organization that helps the homeless isn't something you have to do every week, or on a regular basis.

What Will I Do? Most organizations will use you to help prepare food, organize an event, or help with the event's setup and cleanup.

Whom Will I Work With? A few adults, mostly. Homeless shelters are sometimes really big centers that require employees working full-time to keep them going. So some adults you'll run into might work there full-time. Others are just lending a hand.

Can Money Help Out? Yes. Try using your money to whip up something called a car-kit. Get a Tupperware box and fill it with the essentials it would take to keep clean and safe if you lived on the street, like soap, a toothbrush, tissues or toilet paper, or a hairbrush. Then get a list of homeless shelters in your area that have toll-free numbers and include that in the car-kit too. Encourage your parents or youth group to plan a day to distribute the kits.

Lack of Food Resources

What's It All About? Not having the things it takes to stay healthy and educated, like food, schoolbooks, or school supplies.

How Many Hours Does It Take? As little as one to two hours per week, anytime you can swing it. Offering your time to an organization like your local food bank isn't something you have to do every week, or on a regular basis.

What Will I Do? Sort food items for storage. Pack boxes of supplies for delivery to needy people. Telephone or talk to people about donating supplies to the organization.

Whom Will I Work With? A few adults, mostly. Because food banks are all about organizing and distributing food, you'll work with adults to get everything coordinated.

Can Money Help Out? Yes. Organizations that provide resources like food, books, or supplies always need donations. You can buy any kind of supply that the organization needs and then donate it so it can be used to help others. You can even do this in just a few clicks on the Web. Check out the Web site of your local grocery store to order supplies online. Then just put the organization's address as the spot you want all the supplies delivered.

If you're working right now, or have a job coming up, consider putting some money aside for something like this. The Bible calls it *tithing* when we give up a little bit of our money this way. And you might want to consider trying to tithe on a regular basis. It's something that can keep you on track as a Christian, because you never end up thinking of money as yours alone. Instead, you begin to see money as a blessing—to you and to others you can help.

Lack of Role Models

What's It All About? Because of divorce and other things that can tear apart families, many kids don't end up with a positive role model in their lives.

How Many Hours Does It Take? As little as one hour per week. Offering your time to an organization like a buddy program means that you're going to pair off with one person. You'll meet up with the same child each week, so it's something that you have to do on a regular basis.

What Will I Do? Hang out. Talk about life, dreams, goals, music, and movies. Go on adventures together. Work on homework.

Whom Will I Work With? Adults and kids. One adult will be in charge of pairing you up with a child to mentor. But then it's all about you and the person they pick. Most of your time will be spent with the child, one-on-one.

Can Money Help Out? Yes and no. Money can't change the fact that the child you're mentoring has no role model. You can't just go buy them a new dad, brother, or friend. But you can use your money to show the child new and different things.

Money can help expose them to museums, plays, art, concerts, and other cool stuff (provided the child's family says it's okay).

Tap into the World

Set your soul on serving people who live in far-off places. Here's a list of social needs around the globe today:

MEDICAL EMERGENCIES

What's It All About? If you're into music, you've probably heard Bono from U2 talking about the problem of AIDS on the continent of Africa. AIDS is a disease that destroys the body's ability to fight off illness. AIDS is a permanent sickness—and it always leads to death.

How Many Hours Does It Take? However many hours you want to give. The best way to donate your time is to learn about the problem. When people in other parts of the world need medical help, it can be hard to get because people like us don't even know anything is wrong.

What Will I Do? Read and react. Maybe put together a presentation at your church to get your friends involved. Then see what you guys can do as a team. Check out www.one.org for up-to-date information.

Whom Will I Work With? You'll do your share by yourself or with a group of friends. Then your efforts will be part of a bigger movement that includes people from around the globe.

Can Money Help Out? Yes. Medical emergencies require supplies. Money is usually the only way to buy those supplies. Money also goes into science and research to develop new ways to meet global medical needs.

FARMING RESOURCES

What's It All About? Many people in other countries need to learn how to farm in order to feed their family.

How Many Hours Does It Take? Not even one. Getting involved with a global project like World Vision takes hardly any work. And keeping up with your commitment doesn't take that much time, either.

What Will I Do? You'll hook up with a child and a family from another country and exchange letters about what's going on. You'll also send money for supplies and read about the new developments you're helping to create in their lives.

Whom Will I Work With? You'll do your share by yourself, from home. But online and around the globe, the efforts of a lot of people will all be teaming together. Check out how easy it is to hook yourself up:

World Vision; online at:
http://www.worldvision.org

Can Money Help Out? Yes. Developing a farm requires seeds, animals, soil, tools, water, and other supplies. You can help financially at http://donate.worldvision.org by purchasing fruit trees, animals, or shelter to be sent to people around the world.

General Aid

What's It All About? There are all sorts of tasks that people need help with across the globe, like teaching and construction.

How Many Hours Does It Take? Between twenty and forty, all at once. Getting global about service usually happens when you get hooked up with a mission trip. So, you'll be working all of the hours at once, and then return home at the end of the project.

What Will I Do? All sorts of things. You might end up teaching, cooking, building, cleaning, or just lending a hand with errands.

Whom Will I Work With? Adults and kids from other countries, as well as the grown-ups and other teens who are on the trip with you. Missions trips are all about group projects and doing things as a team.

Can Money Help Out? Yes and no. Money probably won't be the solution people need once you get where you're going, but it will take money to get you there. If you have to save up to get yourself on a mission trip, it might be worth it. That way you and your money are going toward a greater global cause, and you're also getting to travel and meet new people out of the deal.

Chapter 17

Who You'll Choose to Be

I used to be into snowboarding. But that was before rock climbing totally took over my life. I'm so into it."

"I'm into poetry—like really, really into poetry. My class thinks I'm a loner. But who cares? I just like to write and be by myself. What's the big deal?"

"Church is what I'm all about. I'm in choir on the student youth-group council. I help run our Web site, love to plan events, and I'm always into weekly Bible study."

"I'm all about nothing, I guess. Most stuff just makes me bored. Who knows why . . ."

"Can you say, fashion?! That's me. From head-to-toe I love everything that has to do with clothes, hair, and makeup."

If you could listen to a tape of yourself that recorded all the stuff you've been interested in over the last couple of years, you'd be able to see just how much you change from one year to the next. For a while you might be outgoing, into sports, or love to get involved with team projects. But then you might do a flip-flop. You might start writing more, or listening to music by yourself, or start to enjoy spending some of your time alone—doing what you like, when you like, the way you like to do it.

All of this change is a part of growing up. Each time we branch out into a new idea, it's like a trial run. You're testing the waters and seeing what works for you at that particular age. Take the diary below and on the next few pages, for example. As the girl who writes it grows up, almost everything she's into changes. Not only that, but the changes make her feel different too. The new things she's trying come with new emotions, challenges, rewards, and risks. Check out what's up in her life throughout the years and how she handles it:

MARCH 2004

Hi Diary,

School went okay today, but I'm still so mad at myself for signing up to play softball. I knew it wasn't going to be that fun. Why did I let my friends talk me into this?! I mean, I know they would have thought I was lame if I said no, but stuff is beyond bad now . . . Every day I have to act like I'm into something I totally hate.

Today was the worst yet. Instead of even practicing, the team is all wrapped up in this drama over Monica getting busted for sneaking a sip of beer when the team was at our retreat last weekend. Stupid Gina and Erin kept bothering me about what happened. It's like they refuse to believe that I wasn't the one who ratted on Monica and got her in trouble with the principal! I'm soooo sure!

First they acted all nice during the day. But then, once we were in the bathroom changing for practice, they totally cornered me. They kept asking me question after question and got so mad at everything I said. Then, when I kept refusing to admit that I was the girl who told on Monica, Erin totally yells, "Did you hear that, Monica?! She didn't do it, she promises!" in a really snotty voice.

So I'm thinking to myself, Why is she talking to Monica? . . . She's not even here!

But right after I think this, Monica totally comes out of one of the bathroom stalls. Gina and Erin were hiding her in there, hoping I'd admit that it was me who got her in trouble. What a bunch of jerks!

I'm so over the whole thing. If this is what getting on the softball team is going to be all about, you can count me out!!

March 2006

Diary . . . HELP!

I'm so stressed-out. It's prom time again, and it seems like all the girls in my class are tall, have boobs, dress great, and have tons of guys who like them. But of course . . . not me! What's up? When am I ever going to figure out how to be like everybody else?

The thing that bites is that I'm pretty sure Jesse didn't ask me to prom because of what a freak I am! I know he likes me as a friend, but I want him to like me like that, you know?! Maybe if I could put myself together better, he'd think I was hot . . .

I saw this show the other day on TV, and it made it look like getting myself together wouldn't be that hard. They took this girl and did her hair different, plucked her eyebrows, and took her on a shopping spree. It's not like I have a million bucks to spend or whatever, but I could buy a few things. Like there's this pair of jeans that everybody is wearing and they're not that expensive. And I could buy other stuff that looks like the brand names to see if that helps pull everything together.

I don't know . . . will it work? Argh! Why can't I just figure it out? Whatever, though. I guess I'll just try it. It's not like I have any other great ideas, and I really think I need to try if I'm ever gonna have a shot with Jesse.

March 2008

Hey there, Diary . . .

My new school rocks! When Mom and Dad said we

were moving, it seemed like it was going to be the worst, but things are sweet!! Everything is falling into place at school . . . like perfect!

I found out today that I got the part in the play that I tried out for, and I even get to sing that solo I've been practicing. The teachers loved my audition and thought I was P-E-R-F-E-C-T for the role.

Also, the drama club is going on a trip next month, and Mom finally gave in and said I could go. (I knew all the begging would eventually pay off—woo hoo!)

The other awesome news is that next year I'm going to end up getting to take the AP English class I was trying to get into. Nobody thought they'd let me in, but I knew I could do it. I'm so on my way to college if I do well in the class. I know my teacher will help me get finished with a good grade, and then I can finally prove to everybody that I'm not a flake who's just into singing and acting like a goof all the time.

May 2010

Dear Diary,

So the big day is finally here: graduation. I made it all in one piece, and my friends from back home are even coming out to cheer me on. Mom and Dad made a big deal about it, and that made me feel great inside. I can't wait for everybody to see me walk across the stage.

Amber keeps bugging me about turning down college to travel abroad for a year to do missions work. But whatever . . . that's her deal. It's like we used to be on the same page, and I totally appreciate all her help when I couldn't figure out how to get stuff clicking when it came to hair, makeup, and all the rest of it. So it's not like I don't appreciate her or what she did for me. I guess I'm just over it. I hope she doesn't hate me for skipping out on our plan to take the campus by storm. She's the best—always a total sweetheart.

I don't want to go to college and get all psyched like she is about having my own apartment and not having any rules and joining a sorority and partying and that kind of stuff. I'm way more psyched on getting to travel to South America, help kids, and get to practice my Spanish. It's not like I won't be doing school while I'm there, either. I'll get credit for the work I'm doing. But I seriously don't know if I'll ever want to come home since I'll probably love it to death . . . maybe I'll even live over there one day.

After graduation I'm going to go to the party Pastor Doug is having for all of us seniors who are going on the trip. I'm pretty sure Peter will be there too (which is great since I'll look good because I'll be heading over to the party right after I get all dressed for the graduation). Hopefully we'll hang and have fun and then we'll be off on our big move. It sounds like it's going to rock—I can't even wait!

Voices You'll Hear

So in the diary you just read we've got a picture of a girl who's probably a lot like you. She's into different stuff from year to year. She has to face tough things, like moving, getting guys to like her, and knowing what to choose as a goal for her future. In the end, though, she's on track to head out and explore something she really cares about. It's not like everything's going to be the best-ever once she finishes high school. But she's been through enough stuff and tried enough things to know that she'll probably be able to handle what comes her way.

But before she knew she could handle things and work through the tough times, she had to learn about her world through choices. The different stuff she was into from year to year came with a learning curve. And part of this learning curve was how to sort out the voices she heard around her. Every hour of every day of every year, she had to make a choice about which voices to listen to and what direction to go.

That's the situation we're in all the time. So since we know we'll be changing our minds, trying new stuff out, and making decisions about the girl we'd like to be, it's worth knowing this: not all voices you'll hear are worth listening to.

Do me a favor and think about all your stuff—the clothes, cars, phones, papers, backpacks, iPods, computers, makeup, hairbrushes, toothbrushes, sports equipment, school supplies, shoes, blankets, pillows, towels, purses, CDs, etc.

Next, go ahead and try this out. Count up what you have, and write down those numbers in the spaces below:

Pairs of shoes _____
CDs _____
Earrings _____
Purses / Wallets _____
Jeans _____
Bathing suits _____
Cell phone faces _____
Hats _____

You can do the same thing with other stuff too. First, try checking out all the commitments in your life. Think about all the things you've said yes to or always feel like you have to show up at—sports practices and games, lessons for music or dance, or weekend movies and the mall.

Below each commitment, circle the number that goes with how important (again, 10 being most important) it is that you keep going:

Sports
    1   2   3   4   5   6   7   8   9   10
Lessons
    1   2   3   4   5   6   7   8   9   10
After-school stuff
    1   2   3   4   5   6   7   8   9   10

Clubs

    1   2   3   4   5   6   7   8   9   10

Hobby groups

    1   2   3   4   5   6   7   8   9   10

Church activities

    1   7   3   4   5   6   7   8   9   10

Weekend movies/Mall

    1   2   3   4   5   6   7   8   9   10

Second, try checking out the things you dream about in the future. Think about the years ahead and the way you imagine your life when you grow up—the college you'll go to, the car you'll drive, the house you'll own, what kind of husband you'll have.

Put an X by the choice that sounds the most like what you imagine when you think of your dream future:

College:

____The best—Harvard, Stanford, or some other big-name school people have heard of

____Probably just a four-year college that's close to my house

____Junior college

____College? . . . Whatever

Car:

____Something new and cool, like a Ford Expedition or Volkswagen Bug

____Something that's used but works fine

____Parents' hand-me-down

____Car? . . . Whatever

House:

____Big, and located in a neighborhood that's upscale

____Medium, and located someplace safe

____Small, and located anywhere

____House? . . . Whatever

Husband:

    ____Hot. Nice too. But hot.

    ____Nice, cool, and kinda hot

    ____Just cool

    ____Husband? . . . Whatever

Now that your wrist is cramping from filling in so many blanks, let's think about the big picture. If you're a girl who's growing up, who are you going to listen to? What voices have you given your time to already? What voices are you hearing when it comes to your future?

When it comes to our stuff, most of us have more than we need. Almost every girl has a ton of clothes, shoes, and other accessories. But what girls don't think about that often is the voice behind all this stuff. For example, why do we think we need to have a certain brand name? Why do we think that it's lame to have only a few shoes instead of buying a pair to match every outfit? Well, here it is: we listen to the voice of our culture. We see and talk about celebrities and what they look like a lot. When we try to copy any of this, we're listening to the voice of our culture. We're listening to a voice that is focused on stuff.

This voice isn't a big deal all by itself. But sometimes girls skip right over their souls and go straight for the stuff, instead. They hear the voice of culture and try to listen up. They buy stuff as a way to show who they are or what they'd like to be, instead of showing their true selves. It's almost like a costume party that never ends.

When it comes to our commitments, many girls get lost in saying yes. We end up being busy from sunrise to sunset with things we've promised to show up for. A life like this can turn you into a stress case. You'll eventually become seriously cranky or end up just feeling worn-out all the time. What makes things worse is that you might not feel like its okay to say no. You worry that you're letting people down if you say no. You worry that you're getting people mad at you if you say no. And you worry that you'll cause things to collapse in your life if you don't show up or say yes.

So what's the voice that's speaking to you when you feel like this? It's the voice of achievement. Think about it . . . what person goes around bragging that they're the world's laziest person who's never finished anything or ever achieved any of their goals? Everybody knows that people are supposed to do amazing things with their lives. We're supposed to grow up, get famous (or at least make a lot of money), and make a mark on the world by doing something that rocks.

So when girls catch themselves listening to the voice of achievement, there's a good chance that they've overbooked their lives. There's a good chance they've got a schedule filled to the brim with stuff that's supposed to make them great. The only problem? A schedule this full usually makes a girl feel tired—like there's no room for her soul because her schedule is just too packed to fit it in.

When it comes to your future, the voice of desire is often shouting to get your attention. Because many girls don't really know where they fit in, they've listened to the voice of desire, and they've created a future full of stuff that's supposed to fix this problem.

Are you going to listen to your soul and let it take you toward things that you love? Or are you going to worry that you're not worth enough in today's world?

The Way You'll Grow

Being a teen is a big job. Right now you're in the warm-up period for living a full-blown, grown-up life as a woman. The choices you make and the voices you listen to are like trial runs. They show you a little bit about what it would be like to follow one path or the other.

Take the girl we met in the diary, for example. In the first entry, we see a girl who's trying to figure out friendship and having a miserable time playing sports in the meantime. But by the end, we're reading about a girl who's tried enough things to find something she's really psyched to commit to. It's not a choice that listens to the voice of desire—she doesn't want to skip out on her dream to do the girl-power thing and move out and on to college just yet. She doesn't want to try to find herself through buying things. And she isn't getting pulled into too many commitments. She's focused on one thing, and it's something she chose for herself.

Guiding your own life, working hard, and being careful about the voices you listen to can deliver you a future that will rock. But to listen to these voices, we have to do two things:

1. Recognize that each choice in your life comes with a set of voices that are asking you to be a certain way, do things a certain way, or have a future that looks a certain way.
2. Listen to the voices. Write down what you hear. Check out what you're hearing, and make choices that match up in your soul.

The best bet for following these two steps is to come up with some kind of system that keeps you reminded of the voices around you. Remind yourself how choices work and how you can learn to find yourself through the different choices you make. A plan like this can bring the ups and downs into perspective. You're better able to see the girl you're on your way to becoming if you constantly remind yourself who you are, what you care about, and what you want each time you're faced with a choice.

Conclusion

So here we are. It's the end, but it doesn't feel that way at all. You know why? Because as soon as you finish this book, it's actually the beginning.

You'll head out and show up at school tomorrow, or go to church, or hang with your friends. But you'll be doing it with a little more wisdom and a lot more questions answered. So you'll be able to make new choices and branch out in ways you might not have imagined before. And as you head out in these new directions, you'll know I've got your back. I've given you the straight talk, all the way through. There's no sugarcoating here—just real information and real advice for real girls living real lives.

Real life today means twenty-first-century perspectives. Desires and temptations to have sex, be physical, or grow up fast are real. Worries over weight, popularity, wealth, or success are real. Broken families split by divorce, dysfunction, or abuse are real. Confusion over what to do, whom to ask, or where to turn is real.

But what else is real in the twenty-first century? Independence is real. A girl today has every opportunity ahead of her. This can bring a bit of pressure and sometimes cause you stress, but even with these downers, it's most definitely the best century ever to be a girl. You can choose to practice your religion. You can speak your mind to the world. You have choice, freedom, and the ability to be yourself.

In order to make good on all these opportunities, girls have to understand the real deal. No ignoring the big picture. No tuning-out allowed. Instead, girls can take hold of the way they grow into womanhood by seeing themselves as a three-part package: mind, body, soul. What does taking hold of this three-part package mean in the life of a girl? It means focusing on each part of yourself, equally.

When it comes to your mind, you can take hold by taking yourself seriously. Whether you're madly in love or totally bummed out, taking hold of your mind is about paying attention. You can tune in to your self-esteem, the pressures around you, or the disorders you may be experiencing. By doing this, you're putting the truth of your life out in front of you. Once it's out in front of you, you can look at this truth and review it. Only then can a girl get a good idea about the things she'd like to keep and the parts she'd like to change.

For your body, taking hold means being honest with feelings, questions, and curiosities. Taking hold of your body means paying attention to the way you're developing. It means paying attention to the outside of your body as it develops from a little girl to a full-grown woman. But it also means paying attention to the inside too. Pay attention to the feelings that go with your physical development: feelings about body image, the way you look, sexuality, health, and your changing appearance.

Big Myth: I can shape who I become by what I buy, wear, or have.

Real Deal: I can't shape who I become unless I use my soul to guide me.

Taking hold of your soul is the third part of the package. Your mind keeps you balanced, and your body keeps you running, but your soul is your center. Your soul is like your compass. When you pay attention to it, you're pointed in the right direction. You get a sense that you're traveling on a path that will get you somewhere. Part of the reason your soul works this way is because your soul is where you end up getting deep when it comes to God. This relationship will guide your choices and shape your life.

Other relationships that come from the soul can do the same. Relationships you form with friends or with others through service can develop the deepest parts of yourself. They can help you grow. Relationships you form with your family can also strengthen your center. Knowing who you are by relating to those who are closest to you can teach you about yourself and your history.

Of course, thinking of yourself as a mind-body-soul package isn't necessarily the norm. It can be tough to get used to thinking this way if you haven't tried it before. And the big deal after getting your mind set on understanding yourself as a three-part package is learning to understand how all the parts relate. Your soul guides your life and directs you toward what you care about. Your mind kicks in and tries to handle the things you've taken on and are trying to do. And your body is the machine that helps you get it all done. This relationship goes the opposite direction too. When your body feels run-down or ill, it could be because your mind is overwhelmed. And if you can't seem to get your head straight about a situation after a long time, you can feel your soul starting to slip away, or begin to lose touch with your center.

So as you make your way in the world, just know this: there aren't any easy answers. Growing into womanhood, finding your center, and staying true to yourself is a full-time job, but every girl's been there. And no matter where you are in the process, you're right where you should be.

LIVE FROM THE REVOLVE TOUR

CHAD EASTHAM, JENNA LUCADO, AND AUSTIN GUTWEIN!

Chad has a knack for helping teenagers figure each other out. His new book, *Guys Are Waffles, Girls Are Spaghetti* breaks down the differences in the sexes in a humorous but honest way. Based on the best-selling book for adults by Bill and Pam Farrel, this book for teens helps guys and girls value their differences so they can build healthy relationships with the "alien gender."

Follow Chad on Twitter: @chadeastham
Find Chad on Facebook: Search "Chad Eastham"

A Revolve conference favorite, Jenna Lucado teamed up with her dad, Max Lucado, to write her first book, *Redefining Beautiful*—a fresh perspective for girls on what they need to live a life of peace, joy, and confidence. Jenna invites girls to clear their closets of all the accessories they think are essential and replace them with the only thing that will truly give them the security they are looking for: God's love.

Inspired by the needs of kids half way around the world, nine-year-old Austin started the organization Hoops for Hope which uses basketball shoot-a-thons to raise money for orphans in Zambia. Now a teenager, Austin is inspiring other kids to take action and make a difference in his new book *Take Your Best Shot*. The book includes tons of ideas for ways kids of any age can get involved in their community and the world!

Follow Austin on Twitter: @austingutwein
Find Austin on Facebook: Search "Austin Gutwein"

WWW.REVOLVETOUR.COM